Epping Forest through the ages

by
Georgina Green

1982, Reprinted 1983, 1987, 1991, Updated reprint 1996.
Published privately by the author from
24 Henry's Walk, Hainault, Ilford, Essex IG6 2NR

© Georgina Green 1982
ISBN 0 9507915 0 4

Photographs by the author unless otherwise stated
Maps by Georgina Green and Alan Goldsmith
Designed by Alan Goldsmith

Printed by 20/20 Publications.
Langston Road, Loughton, Essex IG10 3TQ.

Preface

On 6th May 1882 Queen Victoria visited High Beach where she declared "it gives me the greatest satisfaction to dedicate this beautiful Forest to the use and enjoyment of my people for all time". This royal visit was greeted with great enthusiasm by the thousands of people who came to see their Queen when she passed by, as their forefathers had done for other sovereigns down through the ages.

My purpose in writing this little book is to tell how the ordinary people have used Epping Forest in the past, but came to enjoy it only in more recent times. I hope to give the reader a glimpse of what life was like for those who have lived here throughout the ages and how, by using the Forest, they have physically changed it over the centuries. The Romans, Saxons and Normans have each played their part, while the Forest we know today is one of the few surviving examples of Medieval woodland management. The Tudor monarchs and their courtiers frequently visited the Forest, while in the 18th century the grandeur of Wanstead House attracted sight-seers from far and wide. The common people, meanwhile, were mostly poor farm labourers who were glad of the free produce they could obtain from the Forest. None of the Forest ponds are natural, some of them having been made accidentally when sand and gravel were extracted, while others were made by Man for a variety of reasons. The coming of stage-coaches and the consequent building of roads started a process of dissecting the Forest which still continues today. Indeed the last century has seen a great many changes, although my narrative finishes with Queen Victoria's visit in 1882.

This is not intended to be a scholarly work, nor do I claim that it is a complete history. However, I hope that by researching as widely as possible I have portrayed an accurate yet interesting picture. I would particularly like to acknowledge use of the *Victoria County History of Essex* and books by Kenneth Neale, Dr. Oliver Rackham and Sir William Addison. My thanks go to Ken Hoy, the staff of the Epping Forest Conservation Centre and other friends and relatives for their help and advice; also to Joy Blake who edited the typescript and Alan Goldsmith for his assistance in preparing it for printing.

A map is given on p.28-9 to help locate places mentioned in the text; those who wish to explore the Forest further might like to obtain a larger scale map. On p. 54-5 there is a list of books suggested for further reading, and on p. 56 there is a list of museums and other relevant places of interest in the Epping Forest area.

Georgina Green

The larger peat bog beside Lodge Road, near the gates of Copped Hall.

It was near here that several boreholes were made and the soil samples obtained were studied by C. A. Baker, P. A. Moxey and P. M. Oxford. They were able to analyse the pollen content of the samples and work out which species of trees were growing in the vicinity at different points in time.

Epping Forest through the Ages

Most people, if asked who were the earliest residents in the Epping Forest area, would probably tell of the Iron Age earthworks at Ambresbury Banks, and might also mention that here Queen Boadicea made her last stand against the Roman army. But they would be wrong. There is evidence of much earlier people who came to Epping Forest in Mesolithic times, something like 8,000 B.C., and made a shelter near High Beach.

The last ice sheet which covered northern Europe reached its climax around 18,000 B.C., stopping across England in the area of the Forest and leaving many interesting geological formations which still affect the contours of the land and the vegetation which it can support today. As the ice receded the first plants re-colonised the area and soon birch, aspen and probably sallow groves could be seen among the tundra. Gradually, as the climate improved, the woods became continuous so that by Mesolithic, or Middle Stone-Age, times birch and pine trees were abundant with some hazel, aspen and alder, covering the whole area where the soil was suitable. Later oak and elm trees started to appear in the woodland with an increasing number of limes. (This was the small-leaved lime, not to be confused with the hybrid common lime with which we are familiar today).

As the weather became warmer early Man began to spread from Africa into Europe and some continued slowly northwards across the land bridge linking England with the Continent. Groups of these early people wandered around, hunting, fishing and gathering such vegetable food as they could find. They had not yet discovered the secret of cultivating their own crops and so had a nomadic existence, making a temporary shelter when they found an abundance of food. Archaeological research has uncovered evidence of such a site near High Beach. Many humanly worked flints have been found with one or two fragments of pottery, and the identification of stake holes in the ground suggests that some kind of shelter was erected while the flint tools were being prepared. In fact there is evidence of much earlier Man hunting similarly in both the Lea and Roding valleys, where flint tools something like 150,000 years old have been found. Then, in one of the sub-tropical phases between Ice Ages, animals like the elephant, rhinoceros and hippopotamus would have been found, but our Mesolithic group near High Beach would have hunted wild boar, red and roe deer and the wild ancestors of our domestic cattle. They would also have obtained food by fishing and wildfowling in the river valleys; the

Lea valley would have been ideal for this being rather like an overgrown swamp at that time. Other Mesolithic sites have been identified at Waltham Abbey and Broxbourne, further up the Lea valley.

These early people probably travelled in small family groups and would not have greatly affected the vegetation of the Forest. As time went by and the climate improved the pine, birch and hazel declined while alder and lime trees increased rapidly. By 5,500 B.C., when the English Channel was formed, the climate was supposed to have been at least as warm as it is at present, and comparatively dry, although it soon became wetter. An analysis of the trees in Epping Forest between 5,000-3,000 B.C. might have shown approximately two-thirds of the trees as limes, one-sixth oak, one-twelfth beech and the remainder could have included hazel, elm, alder and small amounts of birch and pine. However, at that time there was no limit to the extent of the trees on suitable soil and Epping Forest as a specific unit did not exist.

Gradually Neolithic, or New Stone-Age, people came with more advanced technology. They had now discovered how to cultivate their own crops and so started to fell trees to make clearings. They used polished-stone axes which are, in fact, most effective and compare favourably with metal ones. They chose the most fertile lands on the river banks and allowed their domesticated animals to graze nearby. Although no specific evidence of their existence in this area has yet been discovered, two possible Neolithic trackways have been identified. Pollen analysis in the Lodge Road peat bog, near the gates of Copped Hall, indicates that the bog must have been formed around 2,340 B.C., possibly by the creation of a path on a wooden causeway.

The second trackway has no such scientific evidence, but is nevertheless an interesting theory. During the Ice Age large boulders of puddingstone (a rock made of ancient pebbles naturally cemented together) were deposited about the countryside and in the 1940s a line of these stones was traced from the Thames near Reading, via St.Albans, to the north of Epping and straight on to Marks Tey near Colchester, where the line turns northwards to Brandon in Suffolk and Grimes Graves. This was a vast flint mining complex in Neolithic times and a pathway across the higher ground identified by these curious large boulders would have been a great help to those seeking to obtain the high quality flint available there. Although the existence of such a pathway is pure speculation, it is worth noting that one of the puddingstones is on Forest land at the west end of Puck Lane. To find it, take the B194 north from Waltham Abbey towards Nazeing for a couple of miles and you will find Puck Lane on the right, just after the turning to Hayes Hill Farm (which is on the left). The puddingstone is just lying on the grass verge looking quite insignificant after centuries of weathering have worn it down in size.

By 500 B.C. bronze and iron had been introduced to Britain, but it is unlikely to have made much impact in the Epping Forest area. The poor soil would not have been used by many early settlers when more fertile areas were available elsewhere, and new ideas would have been slow in penetrating to these isolated settlements. By this time something like 90% of the trees would have been limes and they would still have covered most of the area in dense forest. The people who did live here would have relied on hunting for most of their food and they would still have found the wild boar and deer hunted in Mesolithic times, and used the rivers for fishing. Beavers had become common in the rivers and the construction of their dams might well have been a factor in the various flood plains and changes in course identified in the River Lea.

During the second half of the 19th century the 12 Walthamstow reservoirs were constructed in the Lea valley and many interesting objects were found preserved in the marshes. Unfortunately the study of archaeology was relatively new and many of the items were thrown aside and left to decay. However, from the records that were made, it appears that the discoveries included bronze spears and arrowheads, various examples of late Celtic earthenware pots (some hand-made and some made on a wheel), Iron Age knives and gold and silver coins. The discoveries of several boats were recorded but unfortunately most of them were left to rot away. One Iron Age dug-out canoe measured nearly 15 feet (4½ metres) in length and had been hollowed out of the trunk of an oak tree. It was given to the British Museum but is now sadly too decayed for them to display. There were other later finds from the marshes which will be referred to when relevant. The more common animal remains found from the Bronze and Iron Ages include wolves, horses, wild boar, red deer, goats, beavers, small oxen and Man.

Another fascinating discovery was that of wooden piles driven into the marshes to form the foundation of a dwelling above the water-level. Unfortunately no investigation of these was made at the time, although they were found in several locations. It has been suggested that a series of pile dwellings of the Bronze and Iron Ages extended up the Lea valley from Lea Bridge to Chingford. In fact the name Chingford probably derives from Cægingaford 'the ford of the dwellers by the stumps'. How did these pile dwellings affect Epping Forest? It seems probable that their occupants would have continued to clear trees from the river banks, gradually pushing back the tree line and extending the area suitable for cultivation as their numbers increased. It is also possible that these people constructed the two Iron Age earthworks in the Forest (Ambresbury Banks and Loughton Camp) as a refuge in times of trouble.

Ambresbury Banks was built high on the Forest ridge and if the trees had been cleared from the whole area it would have commanded a magnificent view southwards across the Thames to Kent and north-west almost to the Chiltern Hills — an excellent site for a hill-top fort. However it seems more likely that the camp remained hidden by dense Forest and was used only when a safe place was needed away from intruders in the river valley. It seems that this was basically a place of protection rather than a fort from which to fight invaders although the menfolk may have used it as a base for guerilla attacks when the situation demanded it. Ambresbury Banks is certainly an Iron Age camp and was probably built during the fifth century B.C. Although it was hidden deep in the Forest then, it can easily be seen now as it lies beside the B1393 road, south of Epping, nearly opposite the turn-off to Upshire.

To build the camp the area would first have been cleared of trees and the line of the walls would have been marked out in the clearing — perhaps the shape can best be described as a rounded square enclosing approximately 12 acres. The people would then have used bone and wooden tools to dig a ditch about 10 feet (3 metres) deep, piling up the soil in a bank 10 feet (3 metres) high on the inside. This high wall would have been reinforced with any large stones found in the clearing and could have been topped by a palisade made from the felled trees. When you see the walls now, nearly 2,000 years after the camp was abandoned, it is easy to imagine how impressive they must have been when first constructed. There was only one entrance to the camp, guarded by two sets of large gates and here the earth was left undisturbed. Excavations have shown that the other gaps in the walls are the result of the banks being pushed back down into the ditch at a later period in history. They also indicate that there was some reconstruction work on the walls and it seems that the site was in use for 400-500 years, until after the Roman invasion. The excavations turned up very little evidence of regular human occupation and it seems clear that the camp was not used as permanent living quarters. Neither was there anything to confirm the legend of Queen Boadicea making her last stand against the Romans here. In fact it seems highly unlikely that she ever came near Ambresbury Banks, but we shall hear more of her later.

Loughton Camp is a similar construction to Ambresbury Banks, although it has not been so well investigated. It still lies hidden in the Forest, off the beaten track, north-west of Loughton. It can be found in the south-western corner of the junction of the Green Ride and the Clay Road at Sandpit Plain, although the area is riddled with sand and gravel pits and the walls are not so easy to identify as those of Ambresbury Banks. In fact, Loughton Camp was not recognised as an Iron Age camp until 1872 when a Mr. B. H. Cowper, who had some knowledge of ancient earthworks, came across it by chance during a walk in the Forest. This is a much more impressive site than Ambresbury Banks however, high on the side of the valley known as Kate's Cellar.

Loughton Camp.

When the two camps were first built they were probably used as a refuge by the people who lived in the Lea valley pile dwellings and maybe also by the occupants of Iron Age farmsteads in the Roding valley. The river valleys were the main routes into the country for peoples from abroad and over the centuries different migrations would have brought more settlers into the valleys. As the population increased and the people became organised into groups or tribes, the camps would also have been used at times of inter-tribal warfare. The main tribe in the Epping Forest area was the Trinovantes who were based at Colchester. To the west were the Catuvellauni, who had their capital at St. Albans. Over the years the tribal boundaries changed according to the strength of the individual rulers of the time, and the Epping Forest ridge was part of the frontier zone. When the Romans first came in 55 - 54 B.C. and conquered the British, a treaty was made to stabilise the situation. This peace did not last long and in A.D. 7 Cunobelin led the Catuvellauni and overran the Trinovantes, establishing his capital at Colchester. He ruled most of southern England until his death in A.D. 40 when fighting again broke out, and the way was open for the return of the Romans.

Romans
The Romans were very interested in the mineral resources of Britain and in A.D. 43, with their superior army of four well-trained and disciplined legions, they soon took control of the south-east of the country. It was less than 90 years since Julius Caesar and his troops had invaded Britain and many of the tribes surrendered to the Romans without putting up a fight,

considering them to be allies against other British tribes. The Romans established their headquarters at Colchester and soon introduced their way of life to the British people who had not previously experienced such a sophisticated urban society. In order to supply the troops and the new shopkeepers it was necessary to build a port in Britain and the site we now call London was chosen at the tidal limit of the River Thames. There was an extensive Iron Age settlement to the west of London at Heathrow where it was possible to ford the Thames, but there is no evidence of a previous settlement in the City of London. Soon many houses had been constructed of wattle and daub, with wharves, warehouses etc., and by A.D. 60 it is estimated that the population of London was already around 10,000.

The site chosen for Londinium was fairly open ground as the soil was not suitable for heavy tree growth along the northern shores of the Thames. The creation of the town necessitated clearing whatever trees there were from the site and larger timbers were also required for the construction of an increasing number of buildings. Excavations of the Roman water-front near London Bridge have uncovered wharves made of massive squared oaks 200-300 years old, and perhaps trees from the southern areas of Epping Forest were felled to provide timbers such as these.

The Romans also built their extensive road network to transport goods from London to various towns and military bases. One such road can still be traced up the Roding valley. It is marked on the Ordnance Survey Map from north of Abridge to Abbess Roding, and the line can be picked up again through to Dunmow where it joins Stane Street. Extending this line south from Abridge it can be seen to include part of Chigwell High Road and Roding Lane North, South Woodford. The High Stone near the Green Man roundabout, Leytonstone, is supposedly sited where a Roman marker-stone had been erected, and it is this which gave Leytonstone its name (Lea-town-stone). There was also a Roman road up the west side of the Lea valley.

In 17 years the Romans had established themselves as the rulers of south-eastern England, living in harmony with the natives to the extent that they saw no need for military fortifications in London. Most of the troops were fighting in the north of England and Wales and they were quite unprepared for the uprising of the Iceni tribe under Queen Boudicca in A.D. 60. (Boadicea, although most popularly recognised as the Queen's name, is actually a mis-spelling on an old document.) The Iceni were soon joined by the Trinovantes and they marched on Colchester, murdered the inhabitants, desecrated the Roman temple and burnt the town. Roman troops who were summoned to the rescue fell into a rebel ambush and were wiped out. Boudicca's followers then surged towards London. Here, at least, the people were forewarned of the impending disaster and many left the city. Those who remained were butchered and again the buildings were burnt to the ground. Excavations at these sites have revealed a layer of ash and other debris which confirm this. News of Boudicca's triumph spurred other tribes to rebellion in other areas and the situation came to a climax when Queen Boudicca decided to march northwards up Watling Street and face the might of the Roman army. The site of this last battle is not known, but Towcester and Nuneaton have been suggested and a location in this area seems probable. The 11,000-12,000 Roman troops were outnumbered more than ten to one, but without armour and facing such disciplined troops the British fell like flies and the Romans had their revenge. Queen Boudicca poisoned herself and the Romans pushed back the rebels. The final defeat of the British people came from famine, as they had neglected their fields during the revolt.

Gradually things settled down again and life with the Romans continued. The towns were rebuilt, this time with some stone buildings, although no doubt there was again a demand for building timber, necessitating further tree felling. Many soldiers, having completed their 16 years of service, married native girls and retired to villas in the country. These were not always big country mansions; in fact most were farmsteads with perhaps 1,000 acres of land. These farms would have been situated on the better soil as the increase in urban population would have made it necessary to increase food production. With the road and river providing good transport facilities it seems likely that the Roding valley would have been extensively cleared of trees in Roman times, opening up the division between Hainault and Epping Forests. There was a Roman building beside the Roding south of Abridge which was probably a villa, and evidence of the wooden homes of the native farmers has been revealed by aerial photography.

There are also two locations in the present area of Epping Forest which are known to have been the sites of Roman buildings. The remains of a villa have been found in Wanstead Park where a number of Roman bricks and tiles were discovered in the north-west bank of Perch Pond, and a mosaic pavement was uncovered nearby. In the north of the Forest the site of a Roman tile kiln is known, near St. Margaret's Hospital, although there is nothing to indicate this on the ground.

The Forest itself was still largely made up of lime trees at this time, but it had become a distinctly separate entity, restricted to the more infertile soil. It is only occasionally that relics of the past are now found in the Forest as unless a tree falls over, exposing the soil beneath its roots, there is no disturbance to the Forest floor. However, finds have been made from areas now outside the Forest limit and the Walthamstow Museum (see p. 56) has a Roman grey ware flask originally left beside a Forest spring and discovered when that spring was disturbed during the building of a swimming pool in the grounds of the Kingfisher Hotel (now the Woodford Moat House Hotel) at Woodford Green.

As time went by the domestic innovations brought by the Romans became commonplace, even in the smaller villages. The people imitated the Roman way of life and eventually came to think of themselves as part of the Roman empire. Towards the end of the third century A.D. Saxon raids on the south-east coast began and in A.D. 367 simultaneous attacks from the Saxons and Scots would have defeated the Roman army had they not received reinforcements from Europe. Peace was again restored but eventually, with barbarian tribes harassing the Roman forces in Europe, those in Britain were gradually recalled to defend lands nearer to Rome. By A.D. 410 the Romano-British population was left undefended and there was nothing to prevent the advance of the Saxons.

Saxons

The Saxons came by boat from the area between the Rivers Ems, Weser and Elbe in northern Germany in a series of raids, rather than as an organised army like the Romans. They penetrated the interior of the country often by using the Wash or the Thames and following their tributaries inland. After the initial battles for supremacy it seems likely that the Saxons and Britons learned to live together, as the British had done with the Romans.

The first Saxon villages were established in the river valleys, and their houses were built around an open space which in some cases still exists today as the village green. As time went by and the population increased the areas under cultivation increased as they had done in the time of the Romans. However, the Saxons had a less ordered way of life and although the fields were cultivated together, the people allowed their animals to graze freely. As trees were felled the animals would eat the new leaves which grew from the stumps and trample on many new seedlings in their eagerness to feed. This caused a drastic decline in the lime trees and their place was taken at first by birches, always the first to colonise cleared areas. Soon oak trees started to increase as the leaves are not so palatable to the animals and the seedlings are more resistant to damage from the animals' feet. In time the animals were found to be grazing so far from the villages that new settlements were established in cleared areas inland from the rivers.

During the seventh century Essex became firmly established as the kingdom of the East Saxons, a fact which is still commemorated today by the use of three swords in the county shield, since Saxon means 'sword'. In fact, a study of the place-names of Essex is most revealing and the following is taken from Dr. P. H. Reaney's work on the subject. The earliest Saxon settlements have names ending in -ing (people of), -ham

Greensted Church, the oldest timber building in Europe.

(home), and -ton (town), and Barking, which means 'dwellers among the birch trees' is a good example of this as we know that Barking Abbey was founded by the Saxons in 666. Epping is another early settlement meaning 'upland dwellers' as the original site was near the present Epping Upland. Later, as the forests were cleared and more settlements were established away from the rivers they were given names including -field (open country), -don (hill), -ley (clearing) and -stead (place). An example of this is Greensted or 'green place', just south-west of Chipping Ongar. The church here dates from *c.*1080 although there was an earlier church on the site. The present church has walls made from hewn logs. Outside, the axe marks are clearly visible in the wood, while inside, it is possible to make out scorch marks made by the flaming torches used to light the building. The church also has Norman, Elizabethan and Victorian features.

So we can see that whereas during the Stone Age dense forests covered the whole area to the banks of the River Roding, south to the gravel terraces of present-day Newham and west to the Lea Marshes, by the middle of the ninth century A.D. the trees had been cleared back almost to their present extent. The land had been cleared for farming which in Roman times had been well organised. The Saxons however, who had not come under the influence of the Romans, cultivated just a couple of fields to satisfy their own needs. Each family was allowed a few strips in each of the fields which were held by the community as a whole. Their cattle, sheep and goats grazed together untended on the wasteland around the villages, this also being land held for the common good. There were no boundary fences to enclose the animals and they were free to wander into the Forest and eat the new growth of greenery where selected trees had been felled for timber or firewood. Pigs were also free to wander and eat the acorns and beech nuts in the Forest. As the number of settlements increased it seems likely that the animals from one village must have mixed with those from another yet they remained free to wander on all the common lands looking for pasture, and the establishment of this right, even before the Norman conquest, is crucial to events later in the story.

Since the Iron Age, when the trees had been almost all limes, they had changed to perhaps one-third birch trees, a quarter oaks, with lime, hazel, beech, alder, elm and willow making up the rest. The final decline of the lime trees was possibly due to the threat of the Vikings, causing the Saxon farmers to seek refuge deep in the Forest, away from the river banks.

Vikings
The Vikings first attacked the northern coasts of England in the 790s taking back rich plunder to their homelands in Norway and Denmark. In 851 they changed their hit-and-run tactics and stayed in the country over the winter, making their first attacks in Essex. They had now organised themselves into a proper force, coming in hundreds of the dreaded longships and by 870 only Wessex remained outside their control. The fighting between the Vikings and the West Saxons under their leader, Alfred, favoured first one side and then the other until Alfred pushed back the Vikings north of the Thames. In 886 the rivers Thames and Lea became the boundary between the two sides, with the Saxons to the south and west and the Vikings taking control of Essex.

Ten years later the Vikings hauled their ships up the River Lea and made a military base near Hertford. Alfred took up positions on either side of the river and cut off their line of retreat, leaving the Vikings to abandon their position and their ships and withdraw across land. The Saxons brought the captured ships back to London down the Lea valley. As already mentioned, many finds were made in the Walthamstow marshes during the construction of the reservoirs and these included a ninth century sword of Norwegian pattern and several pieces of Anglo-Saxon jewellery. One can imagine the horror of the local people at seeing the highly-painted ships with their coloured sails going up the Lea and appreciate that during this time they must often have driven their animals deep into the Forest. However, the Vikings had little lasting influence in this area which still remained predominantly Saxon under the Viking Danelaw.

By the 11th century Essex had been divided into administrative areas called Hundreds. As these were not of a uniform size it seems probable that each was an area calculated to be capable of supporting 100 families. Within each Hundred, each village had its own boundary and many of these still exist as parish boundaries today. Apart from the small scattered villages there were a number of isolated lodges and one of these was at Waltham, which means 'Forest-homestead or enclosure'. This was owned by Tovi who was the standard-bearer to King Canute and a powerful man with many estates. One of them was in Somerset and here a carpenter was told in a dream that the villagers must dig deep into a nearby hilltop, and when they did so a marvellous black stone crucifix was found. Tovi decided to take this to a religious centre, but it seems that by divine intervention the cart carrying the crucifix brought it to Waltham where, in 1030, the town of Waltham Holy Cross was founded. A small church was built to house the Holy Cross and when Tovi died the estate eventually passed to Edward the Confessor and from him to Harold on condition that a monastery should be built there, and this was started in 1060. The legend tells of Harold praying before the Holy Cross before marching south to Hastings and how his remains were later brought back to be buried under the High Altar.

A New Era

Normans
The coming of the Normans brings us to a new era in the history of Epping Forest. William soon established himself securely on the throne of England, ruling with firm authority. In order to keep the support of the Norman aristocracy he rewarded his knights with lands in England; for example, among many others Robert Gernon held lands in Chingford, East and West Ham, and small estates at Loughton and Leyton. William also took pains to ensure he had the support of the church which was a powerful body to be reckoned with. While the Tower of London was being built as his headquarters, William stayed at Barking Abbey, treating the Abbess with great consideration.

In order to learn about his new kingdom William ordered that every detail should be recorded in the Domesday Survey of 1086. This massive undertaking shows the Epping Forest area to be largely made up of insignificant farming communities scattered in a countryside nearly half of which was under cultivation. As an example of some of the information given in the Domesday Book perhaps the following may be of interest.

In 1086 the lands of the Canons of the Holy Cross of Waltham held in Woodford (Becontree Hundred) covered 5 hides [600 acres in modern terms] and were listed as follows:-
2 ploughs on the demesne [the lord's own land]
7 ploughs belonging to the men
13 villeins, 7 bordars, no serfs

woodland for 500 swine and 26 acres of meadow
6 beasts [probably cattle], 100 sheep, 50 swine, 40 goats
It is worth 100 shillings.
At a guess the total population would have been about 100.

The terms villeins, bordars and serfs refer to the social classes and it is apparent that the new Norman overlords with their harsher rule downgraded many of the freemen and unified some of the social groupings, making life harder for the peasantry in general. Those in the higher order paid rent to the lord for their lands and were relatively free. The majority of the peasants paid for their land by performing various tasks for the lord and giving him a share of their produce. The lowest of the villagers worked for the lord as his slaves. Most of the peasants were tied to the manor and could not leave it without the consent of the lord.

The farming system was similar to that practised in Saxon times with three large fields being worked by the peasants in strips. The fields were turned by ploughs pulled by a team of eight oxen and usually barley or oats would be sown in one field in the spring, with wheat or rye sown in the autumn in the second. The third field was left fallow and the crops were rotated around the fields each year for the best food production possible at that time.

As well as farming their own lands the peasants performed the various duties expected of them for the lord of the manor. Under the supervision of the lord's bailiff they did the ploughing, weeding, reaping, hedgework etc. on one or more days in every week. The bailiff also ensured that the peasants ground their corn at the lord's mill and used his bakery so that a share of their produce could go to the lord's store. The peasants also had to give the lord one or more of their animals each year, the number and type of animal depending on the social status of the peasant. The animals were still allowed to graze on the common lands, including the Forest, and the peasants' rights to cut wood still applied, but with an increasing population some woodland management was necessary.

Woodland Management

Mature trees are ideal for building timber and the smaller branches are useful in many ways, but it is an arduous task to fell a fully matured tree and almost as difficult to cut it into usable lengths. Most of the wood was needed for household carpentry or fuel, and generally smaller pieces would have been preferable. So it seems possible that even in quite early times men realised the value of managing the trees to provide wood in the size that was most useful to them. Once a tree has been felled new shoots will start to sprout from the stump and if they are allowed to grow they will develop into several tree trunks, where before there had been one. Just as a rose bush can be pruned back each spring to provide a plentiful

These trees, photographed near the gates of Copped Hall, have not been disturbed by Man and are growing naturally, straight and tall. They would provide ideal building timber.

To harvest firewood a tree was felled and new shoots allowed to grow from the stump, providing a new supply every 10-20 years. These coppiced trees were photographed west of the Wake Arms, near Sunshine Plain.

In areas where animals could wander freely and eat the new coppiced growth the tree trunk was cut 6-10 feet (2-3 metres) from the ground, providing a similar harvest of firewood at head height. Pollarded trees like these are common nearly everywhere in Epping Forest.

growth of new branches in the summer, so the developing shoots from a felled stump can be cut back to the original stump every few years to provide wood suitable for everyday needs. This process is called coppicing and the stump, or stool, can go on for many years producing an infinite supply of wood.

However, many of these new shoots provided a tempting food supply for the animals, and unless the stools were fenced off for about five years there was little chance of the new crop of branches growing to any size. Therefore, in woodland where animals were free to graze, the system used to harvest suitable wood from the trees was to cut the tree in the same way as coppicing, but above head height, not at ground level. This is called lopping or pollarding and the stump of a pollarded tree is called a bolling. Pollarding is more difficult and dangerous than coppicing, but was the system used in most of Epping Forest where today there are several thousand pollards but only relatively few coppiced trees. The harvesting of wood ceased with the passing of the 1878 Epping Forest Act so the pollards we see today are very top heavy. In Medieval times the branches would have been lopped every 10-20 years, leaving the smaller branches to grow.

Among the pollards it was common practice to leave some of the oak trees to grow tall in the natural way to provide timber for building etc. These timber trees were owned by the lords of the manor and other landowners who also owned the soil and some of the wood harvested from their land. The peasants did not own any of the trees, but had the right to lop the branches from specified trees in their manor. Because the pollarded and coppiced trees can go on producing new wood almost indefinitely there has never been a practice of planting trees in Epping Forest — when a tree dies it is soon replaced by a new seedling in the natural order of things.

The Forest Law
The Normans had a great love of hunting, and no doubt William frequently visited Hainault and Epping Forests while staying at Barking Abbey. In order to protect the game for the chase William introduced many laws to specially chosen areas, but it was left to Henry I to bring Epping Forest, along with most of Essex, under the Forest laws, some time around 1130.

The word forest was introduced by the Normans and did not mean an area covered by trees, as it does today. It was applied to an area of land which included wild woodland, cultivated land, common land and the villages inside the area, all of which was covered by the Forest law. The boundaries were not marked out on the ground but were fixed by a group of officials who periodically walked around the boundary, listing relevant markers, and this was called a perambulation (see map on p. 20). The area inside the boundary was said to be afforested — it came under the Forest law. If the boundary was changed and the land was freed from the legal restrictions it was said to be disafforested. Within the afforested area the deer were free to roam at will. They could graze with the peasants' animals, and on the cultivated land. In fact it was forbidden to erect a fence high enough to keep out the deer (i.e. to enclose any land) without the consent of the forest officials, and a payment to the king.

In order to administer the many Forest laws a hierarchy of special officials was established headed by the Steward, who was called the Lord Warden in later centuries. At the bottom of the hierarchy came a number of Under-keepers and others who carried out various tasks including looking after the deer; ensuring that the fawns were not disturbed and that there was sufficient food for them all in winter; also that lands were not enclosed without a royal licence. Those who offended against the Forest laws were tried at special court hearings. Small offences were judged by the Verderers and the usual penalty was a fine. More serious crimes went before a jury under the supervision of the Verderers, and the worst crimes were tried by a special visiting Justice who came every three years.

The various restrictions imposed by the Forest laws made life very hard for the peasants and it was in compensation for this that the established rights of commoning were permitted in the afforested area. In fact, the peasants were not allowed to herd their animals in case they should be tempted to drive the deer from the best pastures. However, in order to protect the new-born fawns, other animals were not permitted to graze freely in the Forest during the 'fence month' (21 June - 21 July) so the peasants could graze in the Forest only as many animals as could be accommodated on the village meadows during that month. In later centuries there are many records of commoners being fined for grazing more animals than their land holding entitled them to.

Most of the higher ranking officers of the system, including the Verderers, performed their duties as an honour, but although unpaid there were many 'perks' on the side, and the officials had great standing in the community. There were four Verderers for the Epping Forest area, and as well as administering the laws for the king they also protected the rights of the peasants. In those days they were elected by the freeholders and served for life, but nowadays the Verderers are elected every seven years by the commoners, which today means those who own at least half an acre of open land within a Forest parish. The only other officials who still perform their duties today are the Reeves, whose job it is to brand the commoners' cattle each year.

It seems that by the 12th century the only deer still living in Epping Forest were red deer, so to increase the king's pleasure when the area was afforested extra deer were introduced. Fallow deer from the Mediterranean

MAP SHOWING SOME OF THE DIFFERENT BOUNDARIES AND THE FOREST AREAS TODAY.

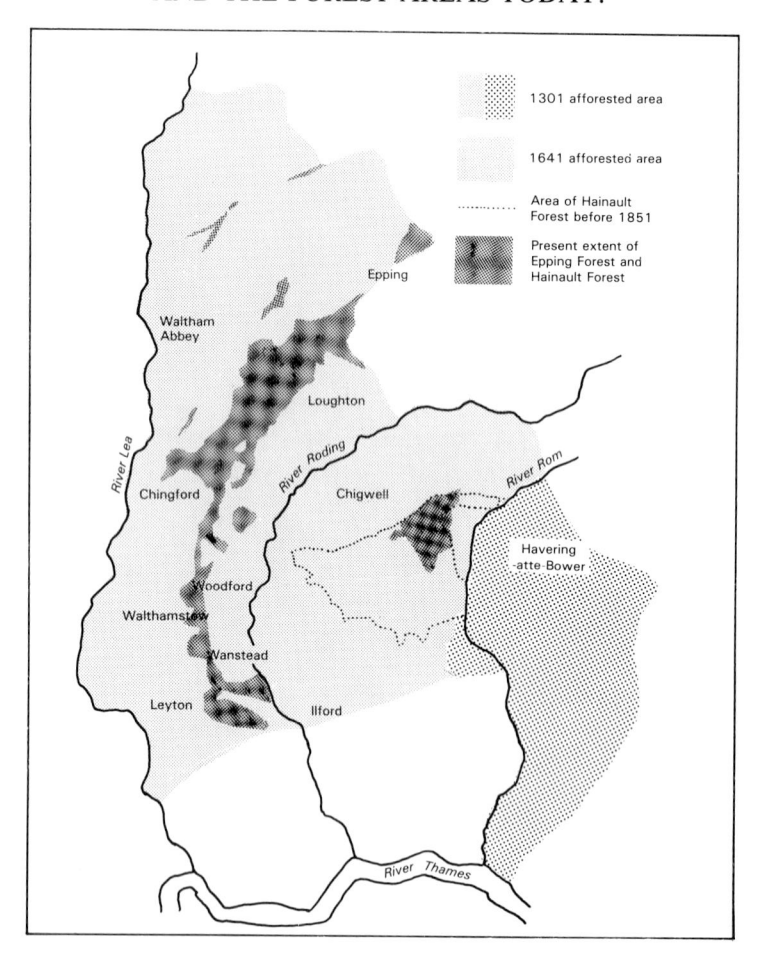

were chosen as these are strongly guided in their territorial range by habit, and will stay in an area without the need for fences. Although the king hunted for the enjoyment of the chase, he also employed professional huntsmen to supply venison for the table, or as gifts to be given by the king. The Forest was also visited by other dignitaries who hunted at the invitation of the king. Hawking was another sport practised in the Forest to provide small game for the table. At this time beech had become the dominant species of tree in the Forest and there were plenty of oak and birch trees. Hazel and willow were still present and hornbeams had started to appear. The wild animals roaming the Forest included wolves, foxes and hares, but wild boar were on the verge of extinction.

During the Middle Ages there were a number of perambulations of the Forest boundaries and the extent of the lands covered at different times fluctuated wildly, but the area we now call Epping Forest was always within the afforested area. The severity of penalties for breaking the Forest laws also fluctuated, depending on the character of the different kings — some being very harsh, while others were more considerate. In 1301 a perambulation established the boundaries as shown opposite and these were largely adhered to for several centuries. Apart from the rights established by the Forest laws the king had no other claim on Epping Forest. He respected the rights of the landowners and peasants and made a worthwhile income from the fines extracted for the breaches of Forest law and from enclosure licences. However, he had landowning rights over part of Hainault Forest and owned other estates which were administered from his palace at Havering-atte-Bower.

Religious Communities
Much of Hainault Forest was owned by Barking Abbey which had many privileges there. In fact the name Hainault Forest means 'wood belonging to a monastic community' and dates from the 13th century. Epping Forest was referred to as Waltham Forest from this time because Waltham Abbey owned many estates there. The Abbot was expected to accommodate the king if he chose to hunt nearby, but in return was allowed various privileges, such as being entitled to send 960 sheep into the Forest. In 1189-90 the Abbey was allowed to turn 770 acres (1,250 modern acres) in the north of the Forest into farmland. This is probably part of the area within the extreme present boundaries of the Forest from Wintry Wood west to Epping Long Green, Galleyhill Wood and back to Copped Hall. Epping Long Green is thought to date from Medieval times when it was a trackway between the Abbey and another small house of the Augustinian Order, Latton Priory, the site of which is just south-west of the Hastingwood Interchange on the M11 motorway.

Waltham Abbey during the Middle Ages was one of the most important religious houses in the country and the village founded around the Abbey had become a prosperous town. The Holy Cross still held by the Abbey was reputed to have miraculous powers of healing and the town became a centre for pilgrims hoping for cures, or to receive help and hope by visiting this holy shrine. It is probable that many of the older paths through the Forest were made by these pilgrims, seeking holy comfort. At the shrine they could obtain souvenirs of their visit which could be worn as lucky charms. The stone mould shown on p. 22 was discovered in Coleman Street in the City of London and dates from the 12th century. It was used for casting ampullae which would have been sold filled with holy water and inscribed in Latin, "Sign of the Holy Cross of Waltham".

The Stone Mould used for making the Waltham Abbey ampullae.

Photograph reproduced by courtesy of the Museum of London.

When Queen Eleanor, wife of the Plantagenet King Edward I, died in Nottinghamshire in 1290 her body was taken to London and Edward raised a cross in her memory at each of the 12 places where the cortège stopped overnight. The queen's body was brought to rest in Waltham Abbey and a memorial cross was erected here too, although on the west bank of the River Lea at the site now known as Waltham Cross in Hertfordshire.

The Peasants' Revolt
The Black Death, or bubonic plague, swept the country in 1348-9 killing an estimated third of England's population of five million people. There had been smaller epidemics before, and the plague flared up again in the 1360s, so that towards the end of the 14th century the number of able-bodied men left to farm the land was greatly reduced. Much cultivated land was neglected so that the value of that under the plough dropped drastically. At the same time the men greatly resented their obligation to work the lord's land when their efforts were necessary for the well being of the community. Many peasants fled from their villages to new areas where their help was so badly needed that no questions were asked. Here they were paid for their services and were able to buy up neglected land and farm it for themselves. Tensions built up between landowners and villagers and these eventually erupted in the Peasants' Revolt of 1381.

Sparked off by the reintroduction of taxes to pay for the war against France, the rebellion started near Brentwood on 31st May and spread rapidly through Essex and Kent. Many of the peasants from manors owned by Waltham Abbey stormed the Abbey and burnt its documents, hoping to destroy the evidence of their lowly status and make themselves free men. Within 12 days of the first outbreak of violence something like 100,000 peasants, led by Wat Tyler and John Ball, were marching on London to tell the king of their grievances. Richard II, having been king for four years, was still only 14 years old, but he faced the mob bravely. Their demands were quite unacceptable and a night of rioting and looting in London followed before Richard again met the mob. This time he agreed to some of their demands, in so far as it was legal for him to do so. Many of the peasants started to make their way back home, but the hard core of militants stayed for another night of rioting. King Richard faced the mob again a third time and after the death of Wat Tyler his courage won him the day. The crowd finally dispersed and a royal proclamation was issued empowering officials to restore order throughout the country. On 22nd June Richard took an army to Waltham Abbey where he declared that he had no sympathy with the rebels and that his promises had been made under duress and therefore counted for nothing. A small band of rebels tried to make a stand near Billericay but they, like others, were soon put down and by the end of the year the situation was calm and the uprising had achieved nothing. However, in 1410 Waltham Abbey was again attacked by some of the peasants from the lands it owned and in 1423 they refused to carry out their obligatory services. It seems that the anger against the injustice of the system smouldered on in the Epping Forest area for many years.

By the end of the 15th century the trees to be found in Waltham Forest were similar to those we see today. Perhaps a quarter were beeches and about one-fifth oaks; birch comprised another quarter and their numbers were increasing. A tenth of the trees would have been hornbeams and there was a similar number of elms although these were later much reduced in number. Willows were increasing at this time and there were some alder and hazel trees. The Forest does not seem to have been greatly used as a source of structural timber, even though it is so near London. Its very existence is due to the fact that the soil is unsuitable for cultivation and so it does not nurture many really fine trees. Although the manorial system was declining, the commoners were still permitted to lop wood for their own use from 12th November until 23rd April. (It is bad policy to cut wood in the spring and summer when it is growing vigorously.) One enterprising man bought the landowner's right to cut wood in Monk Wood, Loughton, in 1582 for £20. He spent £35 on lopping the wood and then sold it for £120. However, the lopping of fruit-bearing trees like the crab apple was not allowed as the fruit was thought to be ideal food for the deer.

Wolves had become extinct in Waltham Forest by 1500 but rabbits had been introduced to England by the Normans and would have been present in the Forest along with hares, foxes and many of the animals we can find today. The commoners still grazed their cattle and let their pigs grub for acorns and beech nuts. Goats had always been forbidden in the afforested area, although the smallness of the penalty made it worth while breaking this law; by the 17th century sheep were also forbidden. Although the Crown's interest in the Forest had declined towards the end of the Middle Ages both red and fallow deer still roamed the Forest awaiting the king's pleasure.

Tudor Times

It was during Tudor times that Waltham Forest really came into its own as a royal hunting Forest. There are many stories of Henry VIII and of Queen Elizabeth I hunting here; for instance, it is said that Henry waited at High Beach to hear the cannon signalling the execution of Anne Boleyn

This photograph shows the deer which now live in the special sanctuary made for them near Theydon Bois. The Conservators maintain the herd and take measures to ensure that the dark colouration is preserved.

before setting off on the chase. He decided to make a deer park at Chingford where he held some of the manorial lands, and it was probably at his command that Chingford Plain was cleared of trees, through to Fairmead. Henry already had the use of a lodge known as the Little Standing on the far side of Fairmead and he commissioned the building of a pavillion from which to view the chase at Chingford. This was completed in 1543 and was known as the Great Standing. Originally the upper floors were open galleries providing an ideal vantage-point for spectators. The floors were specially made to slope to the sides so that any rain coming in would drain away. The whole area was fenced to keep out the commoners' animals and enclose the deer park, and paddocks were made near the Great Standing. Sir Richard Rich was appointed Keeper of the deer park, but Henry died in 1547 and in 1553 the area was thrown open to the Forest again.

In 1589 Queen Elizabeth had the Great Standing renovated as a hunting lodge. She may have used it merely as a gallery from which to shoot at the deer as they were driven towards her by the hunting party. However, it was reported in 1602 that the Queen regularly hunted on horseback even at the age of 69, and it is likely that she still enjoyed the thrill of the chase in Waltham Forest, as she had done in her younger days. Elizabeth's successor, James I, was also keen on hunting and in 1612 he introduced some dark fallow deer to the Forest, by courtesy of his father-in-law, the King of Denmark. By interbreeding with the deer already present the dark strain predominated and even today the wild deer in the estates bordering the Forest are mostly dark.

Apart from Chingford Plain, which had been cleared of trees to create the deer park, there are other plains in the Forest which have been open grazing land for many centuries. Leyton and Wanstead Flats were recorded as being heathland in 1199. At about this time the settlement at Epping Upland diminished in importance as another community was established on open land at Epping Heath. The earliest houses were probably on the west side of the present High Street, and there was another group at Lindsey Street where the road turns to Epping Upland. A weekly market was established in 1253 and by Tudor times the town was called Epping Street. An illustration from the late 16th century shows 'Honylane greene' and 'fayrmeade' to be open land. A study of the area between the A104 and the slip road to Fairmead indicates that it has been meadowland for several centuries. It is probable that the pond here was created to provide water for the cattle grazing on the plain.

During the reign of Henry VIII there was an increasing interest in the Protestant cause and a consequent indifference towards the many religious houses established in the country. Some of these had enormous land holdings and vast wealth, although the inmates were leading a less than holy way of life. After Henry was made head of the Church of England he sent out commissioners to investigate the state of the monasteries, which eventually led to the confiscation of their lands and possessions. Barking Abbey was dissolved in 1539 and Waltham Abbey in 1540, although here the townspeople protested at the destruction of what had always been their parish church and this was saved. No-one knows what happened to the Holy Cross of Waltham.

Houses and Halls
The Abbey estates passed first to the Crown, as did all such lands, and some were later given or leased to various court favourites and members of the gentry. The Copped Hall estate was first established in the 12th century and had been given to Waltham Abbey in 1350. Once Henry VIII had taken possession he visited the house from time to time, and maybe used it as a base from which to hunt occasionally. Edward VI, Henry's son by Jane Seymour, continued in his father's footsteps as head of a Protestant country, and his half-sister Mary, by the Catholic Catherine of Aragon, lived at Copped Hall almost a prisoner. The government forbad her to celebrate the Catholic mass, although this was not strictly enforced. When Mary became queen in 1553 the country was made a Catholic state and many, including the rector of Chigwell, were burnt as martyrs to the Protestant cause. In Elizabeth's reign the country was given some degree of religious tolerance and the Puritans in Essex resumed their ways in peace. In 1564 Queen Elizabeth granted Copped Hall to Sir Thomas Heneage with other lands including the manor and rectory of nearby Epping. He was one of Elizabeth's dearest courtiers and held many important positions during her reign. Heneage rebuilt Copped Hall in Tudor style with a Long Gallery, and Queen Elizabeth stayed there in 1568.

The history of Hill Hall at Theydon Mount is remarkably similar. This, too, was an older house rebuilt in Elizabethan times as the home of a prominent courtier — in this case Sir Thomas Smith who was an influential academic of his day. Unlike Copped Hall, the Elizabethan building can still be seen today and is a fine example of Tudor architecture. Copped Hall was again rebuilt in the 18th century, but both buildings are now unfortunately nothing but burnt-out shells.

Another important house in the Forest area was at Wanstead where the old Roman villa was long forgotten and the land had reverted to Forest waste. Sir John Heron, an official in the court of Henry VIII, chose a nearby site for his new home, making a spring-fed pond (Shoulder of Mutton Pond) his water supply. It is possible that the Heron family first introduced herons to nest in the area, which at one time had the largest heronry in the country. His son, Sir Giles Heron, was the son-in-law of Sir

Thomas More and was beheaded for treason as a devout Catholic who would not accept Henry VIII as head of the church. The Wanstead estate passed to the Crown and Edward VI granted it to the former Sir Richard Rich who was now Lord Chancellor of England. On Edward's death Wanstead was the place where his two half-sisters, Mary and Elizabeth, met in 1553 when Mary was on her way to London to be crowned queen. During the reign of Elizabeth I the house was sold to Robert Dudley, Earl of Leicester, and his queen visited him there on several occasions. Elizabeth was loved by her people and several times made a Royal Progress through parts of her domain. Her entourage on these journeys was numerous and their entertainment lavish; and as well as Wanstead House she is known to have visited Loughton Hall and Copped Hall.

The new houses and important visitors to the area made an improvement to such roads as there were, a necessity. The old route from London to Norfolk had been from Mile End out to Leytonstone, through Chigwell to Abridge and northwards via Coopersale. Near the Theydon Oak public house at Coopersale Street are a few Tudor buildings and Stonard's Farm was certainly in existence in early Tudor times. A look at any map will show that the old road stops between Coopersale and Thornwood Common where the Forest is called Wintry Wood, but a pathway still exists there through the trees. On close inspection it can be seen that it is the old road, made up with gravel many times so that in places it is raised above the Forest floor. As it nears Thornwood Common the footpath veers off the old road which has become overgrown with scrub. However, nearer to the Common the old road can again be traced continuing in a

The Old Stump Road, Wintry Wood.

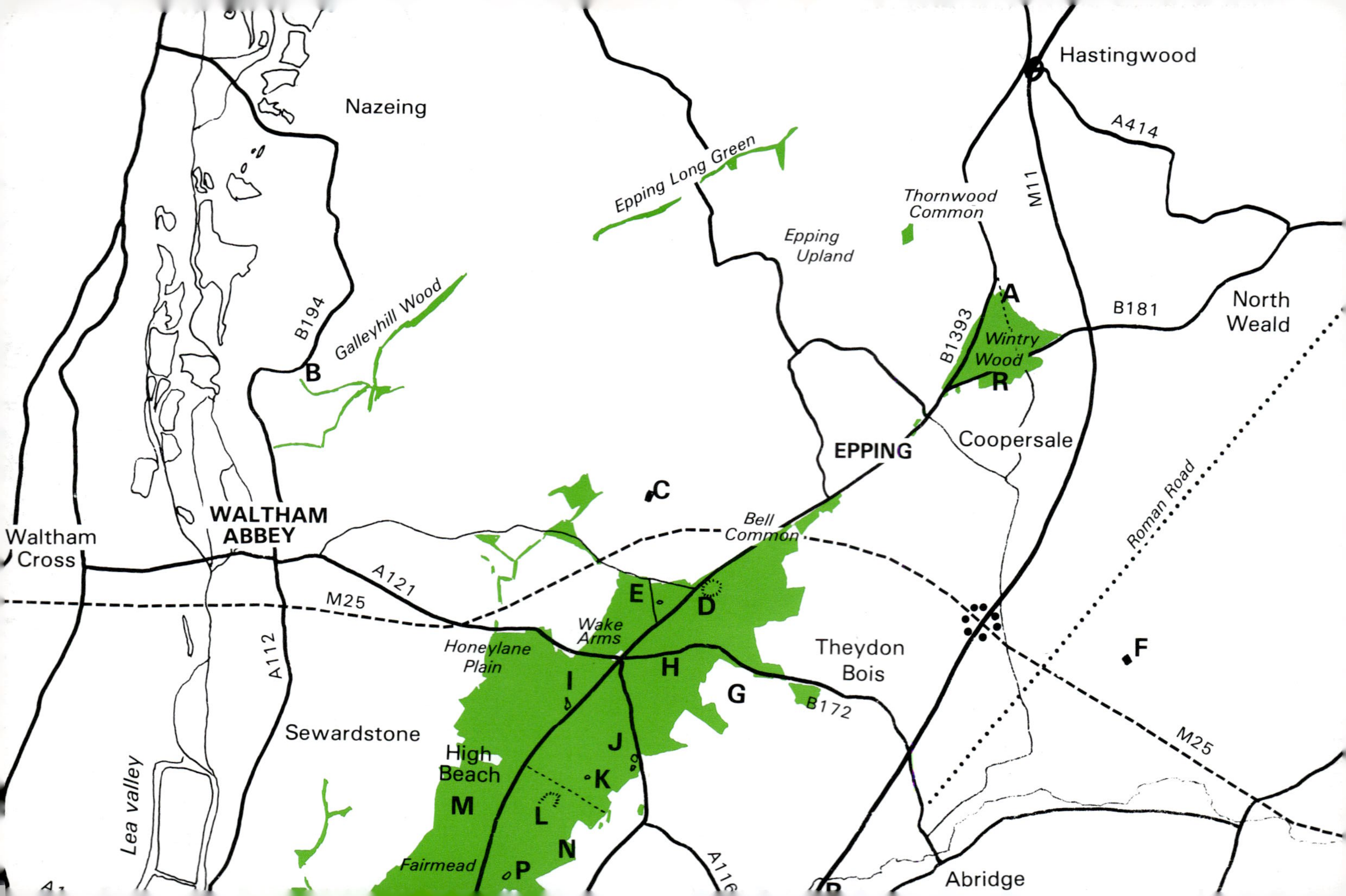
Hastingwood
A414
M11
Nazeing
Epping Long Green
Thornwood Common
Epping Upland
North Weald
B181
A
B1393
Wintry Wood
R
B194
Galleyhill Wood
B
Coopersale
EPPING
C
Roman Road
Bell Common
WALTHAM ABBEY
Waltham Cross
A121
M25
E
D
Wake Arms
Theydon Bois
F
Honeylane Plain
H
I
G
B172
A112
Sewardstone
High Beach
J
K
M25
M
L
N
Lea valley
Fairmead
P
A116
Abridge

PLACES MENTIONED IN THE TEXT

KEY
- Epping Forest land

- D Ambresbury Banks
- K Baldwin's Hill
- K Blackweir Pond
- K Clay Road
- S Connaught Water
- C Copped Hall
- G Deer Sanctuary
- J Golding's Hill and Pond
- U Higham House and Lake
- F Hill Hall
- Y Hollow Ponds
- E Lodge Road Peat Bog
- K Lost Pond
- L Loughton Camp
- M Mesolithic Site
- H Oak Hill, Theydon Bois
- V Oak Hill, Woodford Green
- A Old Stump Road
- T Pole Hill, Chingford
- B Puddingstone
- Q Queen Elizabeth's Hunting Lodge
- R Roman Sites
- N Staples Hill
- P Strawberry Hill Pond
- I Wake Valley Pond
- W Walthamstow Reservoirs
- Z Wanstead Park and House (site)

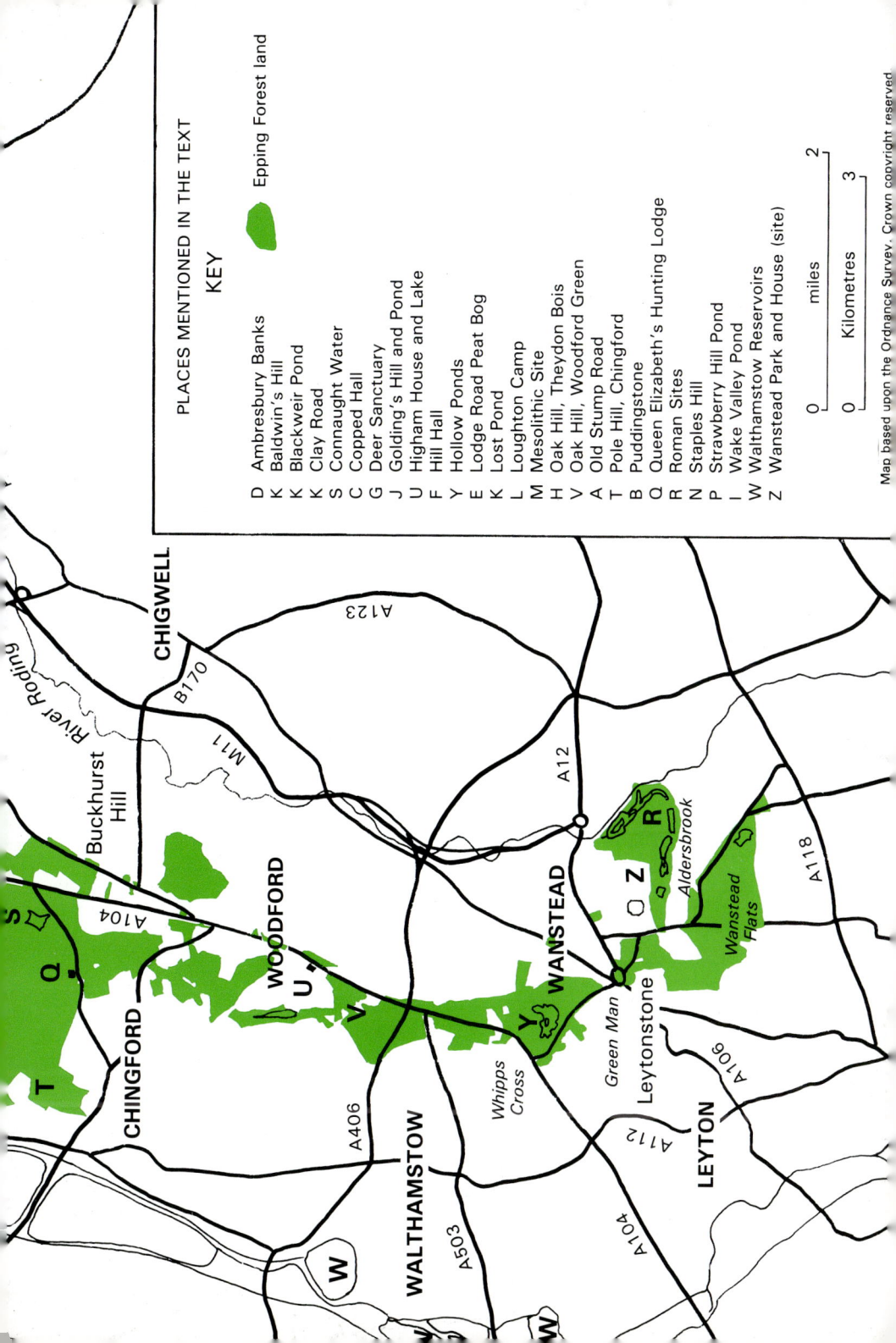

Map based upon the Ordnance Survey. Crown copyright reserved

straight line as a wide raised bank under the trees. It is called the Old Stump Road probably because its course was marked through this somewhat boggy area by tree stumps. Walking its length on a cold autumn day (Wellington boots are essential for this) it is not hard to imagine the pedlars of old journeying to London along this ancient trackway.

In 1519 the road was diverted from Coopersale to pass through Epping Street, and between 1611-1622 a new road was constructed on Goldings Hill, making it possible to travel south from Epping direct to Loughton, and also improving access to Copped Hall. It is thought that the pond on Goldings Hill was made as a horse pond, where the horse could pull his cart right into the water while he drank, allowing the wooden cart wheels to soak and expand in their metal rims which was a periodic necessity if the wheels were not to dry and crack. Of course most people made only local journeys to neighbouring villages, usually on foot, and there was very little long-distance traffic. There must have been many footpaths around the edges of the Forest and others leading into it so that the villagers could gather such Forest produce as they needed.

Forest Produce
Since Prehistoric times Man has used the Forest plants for food. Even today blackberry picking is widely practised as the fruits are delicious stewed or can be made into bramble jelly. Crab apple jelly is also popular, but would not have been made when the Forest laws were being enforced because the trees were protected, the fruit being food for the deer. There was no such problem with nuts which, being rich in protein, are a valuable food source. Hazel has been present in the Forest since Mesolithic times (although it is now rather scarce), and doubtless the nuts, which can be gathered simply by shaking the branches, have been enjoyed by Man ever since. Beech nuts are also quite palatable and can be eaten raw or roasted and salted. If ground to a pulp and strained through muslin, beech nuts will yield a nutritious oil, or if they are dried before being ground the resulting powder can be used like flour. Fungi would also have been gathered for food in the autumn, although with caution, as some varieties are definitely not edible.

Many unlikely plants we see today are quite tasty and nutritious. For instance stinging nettles, if picked before June, can be used like spinach, and the ancestors of many of our cultivated root vegetables would have provided plentiful food in earlier times. Salad vegetables found growing wild in the Forest could have included wood-sorrel, lady's smock and even dandelion leaves, which are rich in minerals. No doubt the poorer women in days gone by knew of these and many other Forest plants which could supplement their meagre diet, but *please remember that it is now against the Byelaws to damage anything growing in Epping Forest.*

Apart from food, the Forest plants also provided liquid refreshment in the form of fruit drinks, herbal teas and other infusions (ground dandelion roots make an acceptable coffee substitute) and more potent liquor. A recipe dated 1675 described how to make birch wine using sap collected from the birch trees in March. Honey, cloves and lemon peel were added, the mixture was boiled and then "good ale" was used to ferment the mixture and make "a most brisk and spirituous drink". In fact the birch sap is so sweet in the spring it can be evaporated to produce a solid sugar! Perhaps a more familiar brew is sloe gin which is made with the fruits of the blackthorn bush.

Another drink which is still popular today is elderberry wine and this is one of the oldest remedies for coughs and colds. In days gone by the elder had many other medicinal uses, providing a purgative, an ointment for bruises and an eye-lotion, using different parts of the tree. Long ago when disease was rampant and doctors few and far between, the well-being of the family depended on a mother's knowledge of the medicinal uses of the plants around her and many of the medicines we use today are derived from those remedies. For instance, it was during the 18th century that the effect of powdered foxglove leaves *(Digitalis)* as a treatment for heart ailments was first recorded, although it had been practised for many years.

Plants can also be used as a source of colour for dyeing fabric and in the past many local women would have worn dresses made of material they had woven and dyed themselves. There was a considerable variety of colours available from the Forest vegetation, all in attractive natural tones which could be varied in shade in the dyeing process. For instance, oak bark and acorns produce a range through brown to black; reed flowers and young bracken shoots give a light green, bracken leaves a brown; heather produces orange; while use of different parts of the alder tree result in a tawny red, green, yellow or pinkish fawn. Perhaps the dress would have been enhanced by a bracelet or necklace made of coloured berries and nuts collected from the Forest. Quite little girls would have enjoyed making themselves jewellery like this, while no doubt little boys down through the ages have used rose-hips to make itching powder.

Apart from these fairly obvious plant uses, a clever housewife could find many kitchen utensils free for the taking in the Forest. Birch twigs tied together and suitably trimmed make an efficient kitchen whisk; on a larger scale birch branches could be prepared in the same way for sweeping the floor. In fact the broom plant was given its name because it is ideal for making brooms — its long straight branches could be cut and used without further preparation. Another sweeping plant is heather, but this had many other uses too. It made ideal bedding material as its wood is springy and the branches are short with dense foliage. It has already been mentioned as a dye-plant and its flowers can be used to make a pleasant tea, and beer. The stem of the heather is fibrous and can be woven into rope, although bramble needs less preparation for this and comes in longer lengths. Although not common in Epping Forest now, heather grew extensively from the Middle Ages right up until the 19th century. It was especially protected in the 1878 Act of Parliament but unfortunately died out in many areas when pollarding ceased and the increasing tree canopy cut out the light. The encroachment of birch and scrub in other areas has also speeded its decline. However, heather is still present along the edge of some of the rides or on the Forest plains and it is easy to see in August and September when it is in bloom.

Another important plant in the home was the soft rush which still grows in wet areas, and can be used to make rushlights by peeling away the outer green skin and then soaking the central absorbent core in some hot fat. Once the fat has cooled and hardened in the rush it can be used as a taper and gives off a surprisingly bright light. It also has the advantage of not spilling hot wax and therefore can be carried around the house quite safely. A similar plant to the rush is the horsetail, although in fact this is in a botanical class all of its own, having descended directly from a type of vegetation which grew millions of years ago. The horsetail absorbs silica from sandy soil, resulting in deposits of very fine grains of this on the stem and leaves. It feels coarse to the touch and was used by the housewife as a pot scourer, or by her husband as sandpaper. The best Forest wood for domestic carpentry was, and still is, beech, which is hard and strong and ideal for furniture, wooden bowls, spoons etc. It is not suitable for construction timber as it does not weather well. Oak is best suited for this, as proved by the many old oak-timbered buildings still standing today, like Greensted Church and Queen Elizabeth's Hunting Lodge.

Today most of us enjoy having flowers in our homes and those who do not have gardens of their own can buy flowers from the florist. In the past wild flowers would have been gathered from the Forest, and indeed the decline of the primrose in Epping Forest is partly due to the Victorians taking the plants home by the basket load. Suitable flowers would have been dried to make pot-pourri or perfumed sachets to put with the clean clothes as we still do today. Larger stems would have been dried and tied together to decorate and freshen-up the home in winter. Some plants can also be used in the same way to keep away the flies, and the common fleabane was sometimes burnt in the home to get rid of lice and fleas. Which brings us to the most useful Forest product of all — firewood and kindling, which was collected as a right by the commoners, as already described.

However, there was a proper industry devoted to the production of another fuel which was also obtained from the Forest. Before the general

Frith's postcard (undated).

availability of mineral coal, charcoal was widely used in its place. It was called 'cole' and the men who produced it 'colyers'. Indeed a village near Hainault Forest which was the home of many of the men who made charcoal became known as Collier Row. Charcoal is known to have been made in Epping Forest in the early 14th century; there are mentions of charcoal burning in the 15th century records and by 1651 the industry was so widespread over Essex that the County Justices at Chelmsford fixed the wages payable to those engaged in making 'coales'. The industry continued in Epping Forest right up until the beginning of the 20th century and was revived in the early days of the 1939-45 war.

To make charcoal successfully it was necessary for the colliers to live in the Forest and they built primitive huts similar to those used in the Iron Age, with a circle of wooden stakes tied together at the top and covered by turfs. The first process in making charcoal was to cut the wood into suitable lengths, stack it and leave it for several months to dry thoroughly. A circular hearth was cleared, about 24 feet (7¼ metres) in diameter, and a stake was erected in the centre. The wood was then piled horizontally on the ground in a triangle around the stake and then upright against the triangular formation to make a large cone shape. The outside was covered with bracken or any dust left from previous fires to make an air-tight covering. The central stake was removed and the cavity inside filled with the glowing embers from the previous fire. The cone was then left to smoulder through for two to four days. It was essential that all air should be excluded as any flames would spoil the charcoal, and it was for this reason that it was necessary for the colliers to live in the Forest constantly watching their hearths, ready to smother any flames with a supply of dust. When the charcoal was ready the cone was gradually dowsed with water and left to cool slowly so that it could be sifted through for the various grades of charcoal. As one hearth was cooling the next was being prepared so that the last glowing embers of one could be used to start off the next.

Any wood is suitable for making charcoal, including oak, hornbeam, beech and birch, but it is interesting to note that the French word for hornbeam is *charme* which is the name given to the middle grade of charcoal.

Social Changes

The Tudor period of brilliance as a nation and splendour in local affairs came to an end with the death of Queen Elizabeth I in 1603. Under the early Stuart kings the country suffered from their mis-management in financial matters, and there was also a revival of the old religious unrest which resulted in the Catholic Gunpowder Plot and the Puritan sailings to the New World. James I was an enthusiastic horseman who enjoyed hunting in Waltham Forest and strictly enforced the Forest laws. Charles I increased their severity still further as a means of raising much needed income from the fines and enclosure fees, etc. He tried to extend the afforested area beyond the limits established in 1301, causing a great deal of discontent, so that in 1641 a new perambulation was made (see map p. 20). Charles I was also unpopular in Essex which was largely Protestant, if not Puritan, because he was sympathetic to the Catholic cause.

When the Civil War broke out in 1642 most of Essex was so solidly behind Parliament that there was no fighting in the county until 1648 when a royalist force was pursued from Stratford via Romford, Brentwood and Chelmsford to Colchester. Here about 4,000 royalist troops were besieged in the town for 12 weeks, until their serious hardships and the news of Cromwell's success made them surrender. In 1649 King Charles I was beheaded. During the time of the Commonwealth it was suggested that royal hunting forests were a luxury no longer needed and in 1653 an Act of Parliament was passed to disafforest and sell off the whole of Waltham Forest. However, the matter was put before a commission to decide on the best use of the area and fortunately no action had been taken by the time of the restoration of Charles II in 1660, so the Crown resumed the old rights over what was soon to be called Epping Forest.

In 1665 London suffered appallingly from the Great Plague. Ever since the worst outbreak in 1348-9 bubonic plague had flared up from time to time, but this was more serious than the other outbreaks and it soon spread beyond the City, causing the death of many residents in the Forest area.

The following year another disaster hit the City of London when a bakery in Pudding Lane caught fire. The flames soon spread to a nearby stable and the burning hay was caught up in the wind and blown against the half-timbered houses so that soon the whole district was ablaze. There had been other fires before in London, but 1666 had seen a very dry summer and with a strong wind to fan the flames they soon spread to the west and north. The fire raged for three days and when it finally died out the whole area from Smithfield to the Thames was gone. The great cloud of grey and yellow smoke had blown north-west towards Oxfordshire, but there can be no doubt that the residents of the Forest must have seen the orange and yellow glow in the sky, and those who sought a vantage-point like Pole Hill must have been horrified to see for themselves the Great Fire raging. At a time when a fair proportion of the Forest firewood and charcoal was sold in London, one can speculate that some may have fuelled that bakery oven in Pudding Lane.

The periods 1652-4, 1664-7 and 1672-4 saw England at war with the Dutch and after 1688 when William of Orange was declared King of England the Anglo-Dutch fleet fought against the French. Although Epping Forest, being on less fertile soil, was not a vast source of structural timber, the necessity for building frigates meant that many trees were felled, and after the best timber had gone, the second-best supply was taken for ship repairs. The felled tree trunks were taken to the River Roding and floated down to the Thames where they could be towed upstream to the naval shipyards at Deptford. Fortunately the Forest's ability to regenerate new growth meant that a further supply of timber was soon available for the navy. Pollarding was still widely practised by the commoners and landowners and as some of the rights were the entitlement of the occupants of a particular house, occasionally the chimney of a demolished house might be left standing so that the owner's rights could continue.

Apart from the charcoal burners few people actually lived within the area of the trees, preferring the safety of the villages. However, after the Civil War the Forest gave sanctuary to a number of discharged soldiers turned outlaws, particularly a gang called the Waltham Blacks who blackened their faces when out robbing travellers or poaching the king's deer. To protect unwary travellers clearings were made along the road sides, and these can still be seen beside some of the Forest roads as areas of newer trees and scrub, with the line of the older pollarded trees beyond — Goldings Hill is a good example of this.

Dick Turpin
Of course, the most notorious outlaw in the history of Epping Forest must be Dick Turpin although even he did not live in the Forest itself for long.

35

He was born in 1705 at Hempstead, near Saffron Walden, and was taught to read and write in his youth. At about 22 years of age he married and set up a butcher's shop at Buckhurst Hill, which at that time meant in the vicinity of the Roebuck Hotel. During this time he became acquainted with a gang of deerstealers who operated in Epping Forest, selling their stolen meat. When several of the gang were caught and had served a year in prison, Dick Turpin joined with them in more serious crime.

They were known as the Gregory Gang and numbered over a dozen men, Turpin, at 29, being one of the oldest. They lived either at Westminster or, as in Turpin's case, Whitechapel, and would meet at a house near the Sewardstone Ferry. They would go out soon after dark in the autumn of 1734, their first robbery being at Woodford, then Chingford and next Barking. They then attacked and robbed a Forest Keeper before moving south of the Thames for their victims. On 1st February 1735 the gang robbed an old lady in Loughton in a more violent manner, followed by a most brutal attack in Edgware and another at a farm in St. Marylebone, all in one week. At this time there were no paid policemen and a reward was offered which eventually led to the capture of most of the gang.

Dick Turpin then turned to highway robbery with another of the gang, Thomas Rowden, and for the rest of 1735 they held up the gentry in sparsely populated areas like Barnes Common and Blackheath outside the London area. From various descriptions it appears that Dick Turpin was about 5 ft. 9 ins. (175 cms.) tall, with broad shoulders. He was not handsome as his face was marked with smallpox scars and he seems to have had a somewhat sullen unromantic nature, without much of a sense of humour. By December 1735 Turpin and Rowden were the only members of the Gregory Gang still at liberty and they agreed to part company. It seems that Turpin probably went to Holland for several months.

On his return Turpin met Matthew King and Stephen Potter and joined with them to rob in Leicestershire in the spring of 1737. They then moved back to Whitechapel and turned their attention to Essex. On 30th April 1737 they robbed a man of his horse and money close to the Green Man Inn at 'Layton Stone in the parish of Low Layton'. The horse turned out to be a valuable racehorse which was traced to the three men, and when their capture was attempted Matthew King was accidentally shot. He was told that Turpin had shot him before making his escape and, as hoped, King informed on his friend. Turpin, however, managed to escape capture again and fled early in the morning to Epping Forest. Here he was discovered that same evening by the servant of one of the Forest Keepers, whom he shot dead on the spot. He was reported to have been hiding in a cave surrounded by a thicket somewhere between the King's Oak and the Loughton Road, but having added murder to his list of crimes it seems that Dick Turpin decided the time had come to leave the area altogether.

Engraved for the Tyburn Chronicle.

Turpin Shoot.g M.r Thompson's Man.

Reproduced by courtesy of the British Library.

He made his way discreetly to Yorkshire and established himself at Brough as a legitimate horse trader under the name of John Palmer. He also established a base at Long Sutton, near the Wash, where he lived most of the time, only leaving to take horses he had stolen for sale at Brough. This pattern worked well for some time but the life of apparent respectability with little excitement from the night-time robberies seems to have left him depressed and careless. In a fit of bad temper he killed a cock in the town street and then threatened a neighbour with the same treatment.

He was taken before the Justice of the Peace and it seems that he had ample time to make his escape, but perhaps he was too depressed to care. Further investigation soon proved that John Palmer was a horse-thief, and later that he was, in fact, Dick Turpin. By now escape was impossible and it seems that Turpin quite enjoyed his notoriety and played up to the crowds who came to see him in prison at York Castle. His trial was on 22nd March 1739 and he was sentenced to be executed not as a highwayman or a murderer, but as a common horse-thief. On Saturday 7th April 1739 he was taken to the gallows. It was a bitterly cold, wet and windy day, but he died with bravado and courage.

Later that year the landlord of the Green Man Inn at Leytonstone, Richard Bayes, published a *Life of Dick Turpin* which was based on the facts available to him and embroidered with many fictitious stories to please a gullible public, and this was the start of many of the legends we know today. It is only recently that the painstaking research of Derek Barlow (see p. 55) has brought the whole truth to light. There are several illustrations from the 18th century showing Dick Turpin and his 'cave' but none of them could possibly be true of Epping Forest. The most likely explanation is that Turpin found a hollow or pit against a bank and, surrounded by heavy undergrowth, this could have been mistaken for a cave when he was discovered. There is such a hollow against the bank of Loughton Camp which is traditionally known as Turpin's Cave, and the location would fit the facts that are known. Looking at it now, bare of any covering, it seems a most unlikely hiding place, but overgrown with thicket, as it was in the past, it could have concealed Dick Turpin and his horse quite well.

The heroic image of Dick Turpin that we have today comes from *Rookwood* written by William Harrison Ainsworth in 1834. This is a jolly good yarn about a highwayman known as Dauntless Dick and includes his ride to York on Black Bess. This really happened some 60 years before Turpin's time, when a man who came to be known as Swift Nicks robbed a gentleman at Gadshill near Chatham and rode to York the same day to establish an alibi. *Rookwood* was never intended to be a serious biography of Dick Turpin, but perhaps this is the way we would like to think of him, rather than as the bad, callous man he really was.

The story of Swift Nicks is told by Daniel Defoe (see p. 55) in his account of a tour through the whole country in 1722-4, which must surely be one of the first tourist guides ever written. It is most interesting to read his descriptions and comments on familiar places as they were so long ago. There was mention of the discovery of a great stone causeway at the bottom of Hackney Marshes, which was identified as the old Roman road. Defoe dismissed the Forest villages as famed "for husbandry and good malt; but of no other note." In the south he was struck by the increase in building in places like Leyton, Walthamstow, Woodford and Wanstead where many large houses had sprung up for the rich City merchants who wanted to live in the country. Most particularly Defoe mentioned the "magnificent palace of the Lord Castlemaine" at Wanstead, where there were "innumerable rows of trees" leading to the front of the house and beautiful gardens terraced down to the ornamental waters behind. Apparently the gardens were so much admired that Lord Castlemaine restricted the public to viewing them on just a couple of days a week.

Country Gentlemen
In 1667 Sir Josiah Child had bought Wanstead House and spent an enormous sum of money on laying out the grounds. The many avenues of trees mentioned by Defoe included one along a line from St. Mary's Church to the Eagle Pond and a few of the old sweet chestnut trees on the George Green date from this time. Another avenue was planted in limes across Bush Wood and this can still be seen today. During the planting of one of the many trees in Wanstead Park itself, part of the Roman mosaic floor was uncovered — and tragically smashed so that the tree could be

The avenue of lime trees on Bush Wood and Wanstead Flats.

planted through it! The mosaic has never again been discovered as its exact location is uncertain. The various ornamental waters were also constructed before Sir Josiah Child's son, Richard, who was to become Lord Castlemaine and later Earl Tylney, started to build a most splendid new house, sited on the present Wanstead golf course. There are several maps in existence showing proposals for the house and grounds at different times and it is clear that Earl Tylney had very grand ideas. His grandson, the 2nd Earl Tylney spent much time abroad collecting treasures for the house, but was in residence when George III and Queen Charlotte visited Wanstead House in 1764.

Like Wanstead House, the Manor of Higham had been owned by Sir Giles Heron in the reign of Henry VIII, although its history can be traced back before the Norman Conquest when it belonged to Waltham Abbey and was called the Manor of Hecham. In 1768 the lord of the manor, Antony Bacon M.P., decided to build a new manor house on the higher ground on the east of his estate. He enclosed some Forest land dropping down the hill from the house to the River Ching and part of this was cleared so that cattle could graze, giving a pastoral outlook from the house. On the advice of the landscape gardener, Humphry Repton, a lake was formed by widening the Ching in 1794. However, the Verderers of that time insisted that a strip of Forest land should be left to the west of the lake, retaining a right of way for deer and pedestrians. The lake is of course Highams Park Lake and is again part of Epping Forest, while the house forms the central part of Woodford County High School.

In 1751 the old Tudor house of Copped Hall was demolished and a new house built to the south-east, in the parish of Epping. The estate was owned by the Conyers family who took a great interest in Epping Forest, several of them holding the office of Verderer at different times.

During the latter half of the 18th century the north of England was humming with the Industrial Revolution and there were moves afoot to improve agriculture too. A gradual awareness of costings, the use of fertilisers, etc., was being discussed by the landed gentry and it became fashionable for country gentlemen to take an interest in the running of the farms on their estates. Around Epping dairy farming predominated and John Conyers experimented with Devonshire cattle on the Copped Hall estate. 'Epping Butter' was acclaimed far and wide and found a ready market in the growing city of London. Much locally grown hay was also sold in the London markets. This success in farming was not achieved without a great deal of hard work from the farm labourers who made up the main part of the local male population. Their womenfolk often worked at home spinning the wool which the clothiers supplied for them each week. Waltham Abbey was a small centre for the cloth industry at this time and the use of home-workers was important to its success.

Industries

Just over 200 years ago the whole of Essex was mapped most meticulously by John Chapman and Peter André (see p. 55) and the detail shown on their large-scale maps is quite fascinating. All the large country houses are shown as they were in 1772-4, including Wanstead House and its extensive grounds. A number of windmills can be found, two of which are within the present bounds of the Forest. One of them was sited on Bell Common, south of Epping, almost where the M25 motorway cuts across it, an area also known as Mill Plain. Study of the larger scale Ordnance Survey Maps of this area reveals the site of the mill mound, although doubtless the motorway workings have destroyed this now. The second windmill, known as the Walthamstow Windmill, was by what is now called Upper Mill Plain on the site of Oak Hill Gardens, Woodford Green. This area of Forest land was first enclosed in 1676 when the windmill was built, and it continued working until 1800. This was a time when windmills could be built quite cheaply and without any legal restrictions. The increasing demand for flour meant that most villages had their own windmill and although its output was not usually high, it was sufficient for local needs. The two Forest windmills were both situated high on the Forest ridge and both are commemorated today by the clearings which were made in the Forest to facilitate their working. Other mills are also shown on the Chapman and André map, like the Fulling Mills at Sewardstone and Chingford (near the present Lower Hall Lane) where woven cloth was taken to be cleaned and thickened. The Powder Mill, which was part of the extensive gunpowder industry established at Waltham Abbey in Tudor times, is also shown.

The Chapman and André map indicates a couple of brick-kilns in the area although several more are known to have been in existence around this time. It was early in the 16th century that bricks came into general use and the lack of building stone in the area made brickmaking an essential local industry. Fortunately there are local deposits of brickearth (a fine mixture of sand and clay) and both clay and sand are also present in large quantities. The Forest was the ideal place for quarrying these deposits and there are many places in the Forest riddled with banks and hollows created in this way. One of the earliest sites was on the north side of Oak Hill, Woodford Green, where Forest land was enclosed around 1607 for the establishment of a brick-kiln and cottage, and so that clay could be excavated. Production continued here until the end of the 18th century and evidence of the industry can still be traced in this part of Epping Forest. Several tile and brick works are known to have existed in the Loughton area, and names like Claypit Hill at High Beach and Brickyard Cottages to the north of Epping show how widespread the industry was. There was also a brickfield on the north side of Wanstead Flats which was later made into a pond. Perhaps the best known clay pit is on Pole Hill, Chingford, where brickworks were established in the mid-19th century and continued in production until around 1930.

The Clay Pit on Pole Hill, Chingford, which has been returned to the Forest.

Study of the Chapman and André map with regard to the Forest itself shows that the area of tree cover is much the same today as it was in the 1770s, although the clearing at Fairmead Bottom was more extensive then. The clearings made along some of the Forest roads to protect travellers can also be seen. Apart from the horse pond made on Golding's Hill probably some time in the 17th century, there are few other ponds shown in Epping Forest, confirming that most have been made by Man in more recent times. For instance, the clearing behind Higham House can be seen, but the map was surveyed before the construction of the lake. This was also before a proper road was built between Woodford and Epping, so the Forest extends uninterrupted from Loughton to High Beach.

The movement of troops during the Civil War had ruined most of the few roads in existence in the country as a whole, and to remedy the situation legislation was passed for the establishment of Turnpike Trusts which could collect money to build and maintain roads by the erection of toll-gates. With the consequent improvement in roads, traffic increased with City merchants and bankers travelling to and from their homes, and their ladies visiting relatives and friends. The establishment of regular coach services made it easier for the poorer people to travel around and in the 1790s Epping was served by coaches making 46 journeys each week. Public carriers were also established so that it was possible for an enterprising Harlow man, for instance, to sell the gloves and breeches he had made in London Town.

All this traffic travelled to London via Loughton, Buckhurst Hill, Woodford Green, then down the hill to Snaresbrook and across towards Whipps Cross. The long pull up Salway Hill was very hard on the horses and the sharp turn at Snaresbrook very awkward for the coaches to make, so in 1829-30 the Woodford New Road was cut through Epping Forest on the line that we are familiar with today. There had been an old road through this area and it can still be seen as a wide Forest ride to the west of the present road, crossing the A406 by a footbridge and passing on the west side of Upper Mill Plain. Its course is marked by cobbles in the pavement of Oak Hill, Woodford Green. The new road was continued from Woodford northward through the Forest to Epping in 1830-34 and the Wake Valley Pond was created at this time when clay was excavated for the road. The pond was then enlarged because the new road acted as a dam to the stream which flows through the valley. There are many other smaller areas where clay, sand, and more usually gravel, was taken from the Forest to maintain the roads. There is a large quarry hidden in the Forest on Oak Hill near Theydon Bois which may have been made for this reason.

Enclosures

During the 18th century the Hanoverian kings had taken little interest in Epping Forest and its deer. It is said that the few surviving red deer were caught around 1820 and taken to Windsor, while the fallow deer were declining in numbers all the time. The Forest laws had become largely irrelevant, althouth the local people still exercised their right to cut firewood and graze their cattle in the Forest. However, with a growing population both locally and in London there was a real need for more food and houses, and more and more applications were made for land in the Forest to be enclosed. The Lord Warden of Epping Forest (see p. 19) had the responsibility for its protection and this position had for some time been hereditary in the Tylney family of Wanstead.

In 1812 Miss Catherine Tylney Long, the young heiress to Wanstead House and an immense fortune, married the Duke of Wellington's nephew, William Wellesley Pole, who then took the name of William Pole Tylney Long-Wellesley. For a young lady who could have had her pick of almost any man in the country this proved to be a most unfortunate choice, as Long-Wellesley led a very dissipated life and in ten years had squandered all her vast fortune. Worse, he was so badly in debt that the entire contents of Wanstead House had to be sold, and when there was no buyer for the house itself, it was demolished so that money could be obtained from the sale of the building materials.

A man who had no scruples about ruining his wife was hardly suitable to become Lord Warden of Epping Forest, but the position was taken by Long-Wellesley on his marriage to Catherine. Under his leadership the Forest laws were not properly enforced. The Verderers found it impossible to carry out their duties properly without the support of the Lord Warden and gradually the area of open Forest was eroded away so that the 9,000 acres recorded in 1793 had been reduced by about one-third in 1850. As fewer trees were available to the local people for lopping, those they could cut for firewood were lopped more and more frequently until they ceased to look like trees at all.

The lords of the Forest manors regarded their lands as their own property and felt that so long as some provision was made for the rights of the villagers to continue on some part of their land, they were quite entitled to enclose the remainder. The government of the day shared this view and encouraged the enclosure of lands in Epping Forest as it was considered wasteful to leave open Forest areas when there was so great a need for more farmland and housing. In Hainault Forest the Crown both held the royal hunting rights and owned the soil as lord of the manor, and in 1851 legislation was passed for its disafforestation. In six weeks some 2,000 acres of fine woodland was destroyed. Further legislation was proposed to allow the lords of the manors in Epping Forest to enclose most of their lands without the restrictions of the Forest laws, leaving just 600 acres for public use. However, there was considerable opposition to the enclosure proposals as it was not only Epping Forest but areas like Hampstead Heath and Wimbledon Common which were also threatened. Parliament had overlooked the use of these open spaces as areas of recreation, much needed by the citizens of London. The Commons Preservation Society was formed by several influential people who realised the need for such common lands for the enjoyment of the public. Due to pressure put by this Society the legislation for enclosures in Epping Forest was dropped by Parliament and instead, its preservation was considered.

The use of Epping Forest as an area of recreation was considerable in Victorian times. The poorer people worked long and hard but on Sunday afternoons they were free to enjoy themselves and they flocked to places like Chingford Plain in their thousands. Here they would find a fairground with merry-go-rounds, swingboats, barrel organs, donkey rides and other attractions. Many people came on foot, walking far greater distances than would even be considered by most people today; others came by pony and trap or horse-drawn carriage. The building of railways to Loughton in 1856, Epping in 1865, and Chingford in 1873, opened up the Forest still further. While the poor East Enders revelled on the plains, the more refined Victorian gentlefolk enjoyed picnics in a woodland setting, or riding in the Forest.

Thomas Willingale

The increase in population even in the smaller Forest villages was certainly a problem. In Loughton, for instance, the population was estimated at 540 in 1763; at 681 in 1801; it was 1,333 in 1841 and had reached 2,851 by 1881. Many of the poorer people built themselves cottages on the edge of the Forest and one of these was Thomas Willingale. In about 1840 he had made a home on Baldwin's Hill - Forest land owned by the lord of the manor. He had enclosed a small garden which over the years had been considerably enlarged by means of a fence of living bramble which was cut back from the inside each year and encouraged to root outwards. The lord of the manor in 1866 was the Rev. John Whitaker Maitland who, as both squire and rector of Loughton, felt that he should give the poorer people decent homes with proper gardens where they could provide their own food, rather than risk their poaching and stealing. He offered to build a new cottage for Willingale and his offer was accepted, although Willingale insisted that Maitland should buy back the land which he had enclosed by his bramble fence!

Maitland, however, had enclosed well over 1,000 acres of Forest waste to sell as building plots on Baldwin's Hill and had made the Clay Road to service the area. In the Loughton manor there were only 50 acres of roadside waste left open for the villagers to cut firewood and graze their animals. The story is well known in Loughton - how Thomas Willingale was taken to court by Maitland in December 1865 for injury to the Forest trees. Legend has it that Maitland tried to get Willingale and his friends drunk so that they would not be able to start lopping at midnight on 11th November as tradition demanded. However, Willingale remained sober enough to go out onto Staples Hill and cut a branch which he took back and presented to Maitland. The court hearing was held at Epping, but the charge was dismissed. Thomas's son, Samuel, and nephews Alfred and William, were summoned on similar charges to Waltham Abbey Court four months later. They were given a fair hearing and treated leniently, but preferred to serve seven days in Ilford gaol, making themselves martyrs.

Meanwhile the move to enclose more and more land continued and the 6,000 or so acres of Epping Forest remaining in 1850 were reduced to about 3,000 acres over the next 20 years. This erosion of the Forest concerned Sir Thomas Fowell Buxton of Warlies, Upshire, whose uncle had unsuccessfully contested the legality of an enclosure of 34 acres of Forest waste on Wanstead Flats in 1852. Sir Fowell was indignant at Maitland's enclosure of so much Forest land in his manor at Loughton and he offered financial assistance to old Tom in 1866, allowing him to take legal action against Maitland to restrain him from enclosing the Forest. Even though Maitland offered Willingale a considerable settlement out of court Willingale was not interested in personal gain and his action prevented the destruction of a large part of Epping Forest. Sir Fowell had a brother, Edward North Buxton of Knighton, Woodford, who was a leading member of the Commons Preservation Society. This Society already had experience in contesting enclosures at court and Edward North Buxton interested them in Willingale's case. The legal problems involved were considerable and Thomas Willingale died before the case was heard, so it was left to lapse.

The City of London Corporation
In 1854 the City of London Corporation had bought 200 acres of land at Aldersbrook to provide a cemetery for the City, and this entitled the Corporation to graze cattle on the Forest land. Many of the City business men who lived near Epping Forest appreciated its amenity value and were concerned by its erosion. In 1871 the City of London Corporation decided to take legal action against all those who had recently enclosed Forest land, and on the recommendation of the House of Lords all other such cases were suspended in the courts, making this a test case. The City solicitor assisted by the honorary solicitor of the Commons Preservation Society spent three years preparing their case which was heard late in 1874. On the one hand the manorial lords claimed that each manor was separate and its commoners had no rights in other parts of the Forest, while the City argued that there were no physical boundaries to each manor and the cattle had always been free to wander over the entire Forest. Judgement was made in favour of the City Corporation, condemning enclosures in Epping Forest so completely that there could no longer be any dispute, or any point in appealing against the decision.

The Epping Forest Act
If the City of London Corporation was to take control of Epping Forest the next step had to be the purchase of as much Forest land as possible. It was agreed that all Forest lands enclosed after 1851 should be returned to the Forest unless they had been built on, or were attached to a house. An exception was made for the land on which High Beach Church stands and there were many who felt that an exception should also be made in their own case, so an Arbitrator was appointed to hear these people and settle any disputes. Legislation was prepared, went through Parliament without opposition, and in 1878 the Epping Forest Act was passed. This Act abolished all the rights of the Crown and the power of the Forest courts, and empowered the City of London Corporation to administer Epping Forest as Conservators, with a duty to keep it unenclosed as an open space for the recreation and enjoyment of the public. Under the Act the Conservators must preserve the natural aspect of the Forest; protect the trees and

other plants growing there, and the ancient earthworks; prevent the cutting of wood or digging of clay, sand or gravel; and resist all attempts to build on Forest land. The Conservators may enclose areas or build lodges etc. for management purposes and also have the power to provide sporting facilities on Forest land. There are a great many other clauses to the Act, but no provision was made for financing the management of Epping Forest and this has always been paid for by the City of London Corporation from its own funds.

Cows grazing today on Wanstead Flats.

Compensation was agreed for the loss of lopping rights in the various manors, some of the money granted to Loughton being spent on the construction of Lopping Hall. Grazing was allowed to continue as before under the new Act and various guidelines were drawn up to define who was entitled to this privilege. The office of Verderer was retained, not with any legal powers but as a representative of the local people, and both Sir Thomas Fowell Buxton and his brother served as Verderers for many years. Edward North Buxton had always taken a great interest in the natural history of the Forest and his advice was to benefit its management policy at a time when ecology was unknown and much of the Conservators' work was experimental. He also took an interest in the fallow deer which had declined to just one buck and 11 does in 1870. Fortunately they were able to breed successfully and their numbers increased rapidly after 1878.

Although the Crown gave up all rights in the Forest the monarch was entitled to appoint a Ranger who would have some control over important matters of policy. Queen Victoria chose her third and favourite son, Arthur, Duke of Connaught, to hold this position, as he had a great interest in trees. He was 28 years of age when the Act was passed and as

The Lost Pond on Blackweir Hill.

the son of Queen Victoria and a greatly respected serving soldier, spent much of his time abroad. However, he and the Duchess — Princess Louise of Prussia whom he married in 1879 — managed to visit Epping Forest on a number of occasions, particularly in the years immediately after 1878.

The Forest itself had changed quite drastically since 1851. Alien trees and shrubs, like the sweet chestnut and rhododendron, had been planted in many of the enclosed places and the trees on these lands had largely escaped pollarding. However, in those areas which had remained open to the public the trees had been so badly mutilated by lopping that they did not provide any shade and the undergrowth became very dense. Some of the first tasks carried out by the staff of the newly appointed Superintendent involved opening up the Forest by cutting new roads and footpaths and thinning out the trees. Many blocked streams were cleared to drain marshy areas and the swamp near Chingford Plain was dried out by means of a large lake which was made both for drainage and as an amenity. It was called Connaught Water after the Ranger, as was the newly constructed Rangers Road. Other lakes were formed when gravel and sand extraction ceased, including that on Strawberry Hill, the Hollow Ponds at Leytonstone, and Blackweir Pond, otherwise known as the Lost Pond.

Queen Victoria's visit
The royal seal of approval was stamped on the preservation of Epping Forest when Queen Victoria visited High Beach on 6th May 1882 and

declared . . . "it gives me the greatest satisfaction to dedicate this beautiful Forest to the use and enjoyment of my people for all time."

The day was one of celebration over much of East London and elaborate preparations had been made for the Queen's visit. Her Majesty was to arrive by train at Chingford Station and this was decorated with thousands of flowers, while a specially constructed archway over the entrance to the station proclaimed THE FOREST WELCOMES THE QUEEN. Queen Elizabeth's Hunting Lodge had been renovated and it was expected that Her Majesty would visit the building, although the procession did not in fact stop there. The recently built Royal Forest Hotel was tastefully decorated for the occasion, and the fences still enclosing parts of Chingford Plain were hastily demolished. The royal procession was to travel via Rangers Road, passing Connaught Water, to Epping New Road and then across Fairmead to High Beach. Here a vast grandstand had been constructed, with a magnificent view across the Lea valley, which was to seat the many dignitaries who were to witness the proceedings. Another pavillion had been built so that the Queen's carriage could be drawn up and she could participate in the ceremony without leaving it.

Although a fair amount of rain had fallen during the preceding night, Saturday 6th May 1882 dawned fine, the rain adding a delightful freshness to the Forest greenery. While Queen Victoria walked in the gardens of Windsor Castle admiring the lilac and chestnut blooms, East London hummed with activity. An estimated 500,000 people came to cheer their Queen as she passed by, some by train to Chingford, Buckhurst Hill, Loughton and Ponder's End, and many on foot. Those who came in carriages were permitted to station themselves on the Forest land a little way back from the roadside, allowing spectators to line the route in front of them. Special arrangements had been made for the local schoolchildren to have a good vantage point, thanks to the forethought of Edward North Buxton, and various stalls were set up to provide refreshments for the crowds. The 1st Essex Artillery stationed themselves near Hawkwood ready to fire a 21-gun salute when the Queen arrived at Chingford Station, and several military bands took their places, ready to play as the Queen passed by. Meanwhile, the many dignitaries invited to the ceremony were arriving at Loughton Station where about 190 carriages from the locality had been commandeered to take them to High Beach. Around 1,500 police were on duty in the area but nothing occurred to spoil the happy atmosphere.

The first royal arrivals were Prince Arthur, Duke of Connaught and Ranger of Epping Forest, Princess Louise, Duchess of Connaught (Louischen), and Princess Louise, the Duke's sister. Two royal carriages were driven into the station yard, their hoods were thrown back, the sun was shining and all was in readiness for the arrival of Queen Victoria and

QUEEN VICTORIA AT HIGH BEACH
From a painting by Neville Lewis at County Hall, Chelmsford.
Reproduced by permission of Essex County Council.

It shows the reception of Her Majesty by the Duke of Connaught with other dignitaries, while little Miss Victoria Buxton waits to present her bouquet.

Princess Beatrice. The following account of the afternoon's events is taken from Queen Victoria's journal, written that evening at Windsor Castle. I am most privileged that a photocopy of these pages was made available to me from the Royal Archives, although the following passage has already appeared in *The Letters of Queen Victoria,* 2nd series, Vol. III, edited by George Buckle.

"At quarter to 3 left with Beatrice for Epping Forest, which we reached at 4. Great crowds all along the railroad and a very great one on getting out. Arthur, Louischen, Louise, and the Lord Mayor met us. Volunteers and troops were out, and everything extremely well arranged. A great stand, full of people, and a very pretty arch had been erected. Arthur rode next my carriage, and Louise, Beatrice, and Louischen drove with me. The Lord Mayor and my two Equerries rode behind the carriage. Drove through enormous crowds, who lined the whole way, nearly 3 miles, to High Beach, where an Address was received, and read, and I declared the Park open. The sight was very brilliant. There was a temporary building in which the Lord Mayor had entertained 10,000 people at luncheon. He hurriedly dismounted, and put on his robes, before presenting the Address, which was read by the Recorder, and I read a short answer, which caused great cheering. An album with views of this fine and picturesque Park, reminding one of Burnham Beeches and Richmond Park, was presented to me, and a little girl, daughter of Sir Fowell and Victoria Buxton (herself my goddaughter), was held up to the carriage, to give me a bouquet... Returned the same way. The enthusiasm was very great, and many quite poor people were out. The Park has been given to the poor of the East End, as a sort of recreation ground. Nothing but loyal expressions and kind faces did I hear and see; it was most gratifying."

Later that evening the Queen heard the happy news that she had again been made a great-grandmother by the birth of a son to Princess William of Prussia, while a grand firework display was held behind the Royal Forest Hotel to complete the happy day for the many thousands of local people still gathered in the Forest.

In Conclusion

Epping Forest has been protected by Act of Parliament since 1878, but even so, the pressures of public enjoyment have made changes, just as other uses changed it in the past. Of the 450 or so different species of flowering plant recorded in the 1880s, one-third have now disappeared from the Forest. Epping Forest today is used for recreational purposes and facilities are provided for golf, horse riding, football and other sports. Some people come to enjoy the quietness, others like to run and play on the plains or under the trees. The Forest is used as a classroom by many children who come to learn about the plant and animal life, and a visit to Queen Elizabeth's Hunting Lodge can be most enjoyable and informative. Whether it is a day out with an organised group or an afternoon picnic with the family, we can all enjoy the Forest in our own way.

But Epping Forest provides a home for many non-human creatures. Most people are aware that many birds breed in the Forest, and could probably include foxes, squirrels, rabbits and maybe snakes and bats among the animals they think live there. However, that is only the tip of the iceberg of hidden creatures who live in the Forest. Centipedes, earwigs, spiders and woodlice can live in the bark of an old tree stump, and Epping Forest is famed in natural history circles as the home of over 1,500 different species of beetle. Some of these species are dependent on trees, needing the wood, leaves or fruit, while other beetles may live among the dead leaves, fungi or animal droppings found on the Forest floor.

Apart from the many common forms of vegetation there are also a number of rarer plants, including the sundew and cotton grass, keeping a precarious hold in Epping Forest as one of the last remaining sites in the county. The Forest also contains many lichens and mosses and other more primitive forms of vegetable life have existed in the Forest for many centuries. There are hundreds of species of fungi, barely visible to the naked eye, which flourish on the dead wood and decaying leaves. They are necessary for the destruction of the old dead trees and for the preparation of a new layer of decomposed vegetable humus ready for the growth of a new generation of trees and other plants.

The fact that the trees have been growing uninterrupted in Epping Forest since Prehistoric times has permitted the development and survival of a remarkably complex relationship between plant and animal life that can be found in few other places. Some of these primitive forms of life have died out in today's polluted air, but others are hanging on in the ancient woodlands, existing together and needing each other to keep a balanced community. If one is destroyed, the whole chain of interdependent species is threatened.

Because Epping Forest is one of very few places where it is still possible to see the effects of Medieval woodland management, and because of the ancient and rare forms of life it contains, it *must* be preserved. Why should we think we have the right to destroy this Forest which has evolved over more than 10,000 years? The Epping Forest Act of 1878 empowers the City of London Corporation to protect the Forest and it is important that we all realise why it still needs protection now. Homes and factories may be needed, and motorways may be in the national interest, but this ancient woodland is much more a part of our country's heritage than a stately home or a priceless picture. We are extremely lucky that it is so near to the heart of London and can be appreciated by so many people. The City Corporation is to be applauded for adding to the northern part of the Forest and securing additional buffer land for its protection. Hopefully this trend will continue.

Suggestions for further reading

Addison, Sir William *Portrait of Epping Forest*
Robert Hale 1977

Addison, Sir William *Epping Forest, Figures in a Landscape*
Robert Hale 1991

Brimble, J.A. *London's Epping Forest*
1950 3rd edition published by Brimble in 1965

Brooks, R.T. and Fulcher, E.A. *An Archaeological Guide to Epping Forest*
City of London Corporation 1979

Buxton, E.N. *Epping Forest*
(A naturalist's account of the Forest as it was soon after 1878.)
Stanford 1884, many later editions

Epping Forest - the Natural Aspect ? **Edited by D.Corke**
Essex Naturalist no.2 Essex Field Club 1978
(The paper "Archaeology and Land-use History" by Oliver Rackham was the starting point for "Epping Forest through the Ages".)

The Wildlife of Epping Forest **Edited by D.Corke**
Essex Naturalist no.4 Essex Field Club 1979

Epping Forest through the Eye of a Naturalist **Edited by M.W.Hanson**
Essex Naturalist no.11 Essex Field Club 1992

Epping Forest then and now **Compiled by W.G.Ramsey and R.L.Fowkes**
Battle of Britain Prints International Ltd 1986

Fisher, W.R. *The Forest of Essex*
(A historical and legal account of the Forest.)
Butterworths 1887

Law, A.D. and Barry, S. *The Forest in Walthamstow and Chingford*
Chingford Historical Society and Walthamstow Antiquarian Society 1978

Leutscher, A. *Epping Forest, its History and Wildlife*
David and Charles 1974

Mitchell, R. *Bob Mitchell's Epping Forest Companion*
Seax Books 1991

The Official Guide to Epping Forest
Corporation of London 1993

Ward, B. *Trees in Epping Forest*
City of London Corporation 1980

Relevant Epping Forest Organisations

The Friends of Epping Forest
Originally formed in 1968, the Friends' main objective is to protect the Forest for the public in accordance with the 1878 Act and to provide a consultative link between the Conservators of Epping Forest and members of the public. They also aim to further the knowledge and appreciation of the public in all matters relating to Epping Forest. The officers and committee include a range of individuals with specialised expertise and representives from other interested groups, all of whom work on a voluntary basis. The Friends publishes a newsletter three times each year and organises a regular programme of walks in the Forest.

The Epping Forest Conservation Volunteers
Established in 1977, the Conservation Volunteers are a group actively involved with the conservation and management of Epping Forest. Members meet on alternate Sundays to work on selected sites needing specialised care. Working under direction, tasks such as clearing heathland of invading scrub or cleaning ponds are carried out to improve the variety and beauty of the Forest. Those less actively inclined can support the work of the Conservation Volunteers as Associate Members, helping to finance the purchase of necessary equipment etc.

The Epping Forest Centenary Trust
The Trust was set up in 1978 to celebrate the centenary of the protection of Epping Forest and aims to assist in promoting, communicating and understanding the Forest's unique character. The Conservation Project Officer arranges for school and youth groups to work in the Forest while learning a variety of practical, social and personal skills, as well as an appreciation of their surroundings. Past projects include the restoration of the "Lawrence hut" at the Warren and the creation of a special wheelchair path at High Beach. A range of activities are organised by the Trust for education, enjoyment and/or fund-raising.

Details of all the above can be obtained from the Information Centre.

Epping Forest Information Centre
High Beach, Loughton, Essex IG10 4AF   *0181 508 0028*
The Corporation provides an Information Centre at High Beach where visitors can buy books and maps as well as seeing displays relating to the Forest. Opening times are different as the seasons change, please telephone for exact details. The Information Centre staff also arrange monthly guided walks in the Forest and a programme of winter lectures at the adjacent Field Studies Centre.

Epping Forest Field Studies Centre
High Beach, Loughton, Essex IG10 4AF   *0181 508 7714*
The Centre is managed by the Field Studies Council on behalf of the Conservators to provide a teaching facility in the Forest, including an extensive library. School parties from infant to A-level, adult groups and children's activities are run from the Centre.

Relevant places of interest in the Epping Forest area

Epping Forest District Museum
39-41 Sun Street, Waltham Abbey, Essex EN9 1EL *01992 716882*
Situated in two timber-framed houses at the end of the main street in Waltham Abbey, the museum has permanent displays illustrating the social history of the district. Perhaps the most notable feature is the oak panelling carved for the Abbot of Waltham during the reign of Henry VIII. There are also changing temporary exhibitions of local interest, and occasional demonstrations, lectures and events arranged for children.

Greensted Church
The ancient wooden church at Greensted (see page 13) can be found beside a turning west from the A113 between Chipping Ongar and Marden Ash.

Lee Valley Park Countryside Centre
Abbey Farmhouse, Crooked Mile, Waltham Abbey, Essex EN9 1QX
01992 713838
The Centre provides information about activities held in the Lee Valley, as well the historical development and natural history of the area. It is situated in the Abbey Gardens, close by the abbey ruins and the fine Norman church.

Queen Elizabeth's Hunting Lodge
Rangers Road, Chingford, E4 7QH *0181 529 6681*
Built by order of Henry VIII in 1543, the hunt "standing" is constructed of massive oak timbers which illustrate the skills of the royal craftsmen. It was acquired by the City Corporation in 1878. The last complete restoration was carried out after extensive surveys in the early 1990s revealing many new facets of the building which is open to the public.

Vestry House Museum
Vestry Road, Walthamstow, E17 9NH *0181 509 1917*
The museum is housed in the old workhouse, built in 1730, in the heart of Walthamstow village. A range of exhibitions illustrate various historical topics, including the car built locally by Frederick Bremer in 1892-4, one of the earliest built in Britain. The building also houses the borough's archive collection.

Please telephone for details of opening times, wheelchair access etc.

A **special path** has been constructed through the Forest at High Beach for wheelchair users and those who prefer a firm level floor.
Contact the Information Centre for details. (see previous page)